ORIGAMI

Japanese Paper Folding

MADE EASY

Florence Sakade
Revised by **Marc Kirschenbaum**

TUTTLE Publishing

Tokyo | Rutland, Vermont | Singapore

Contents

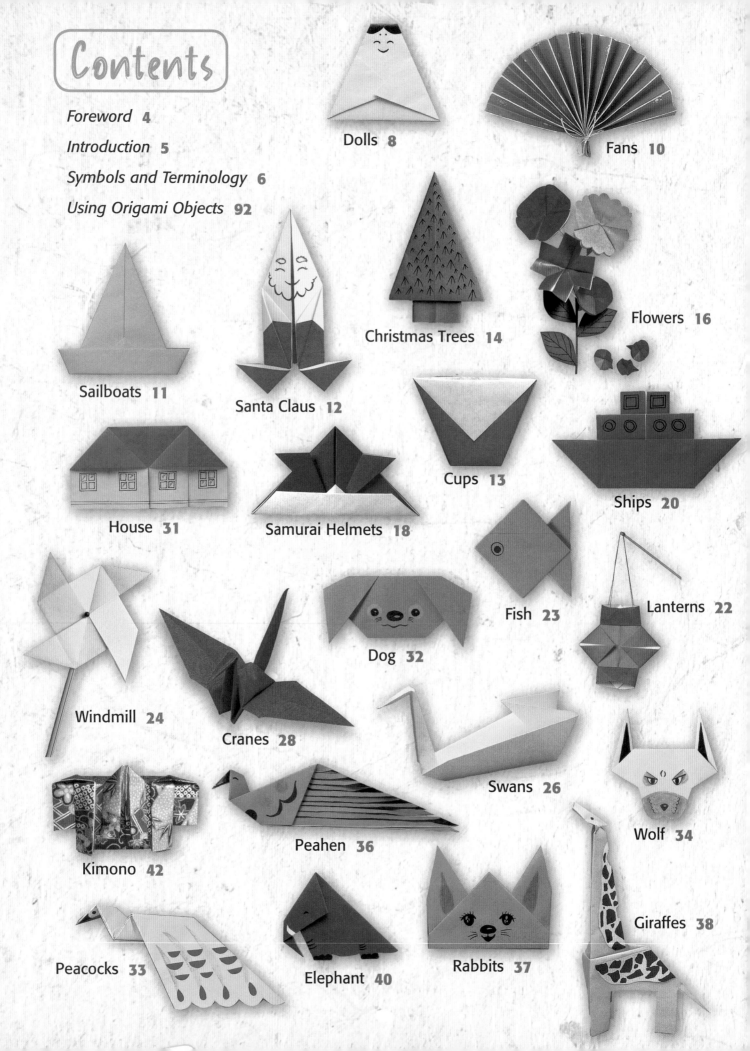

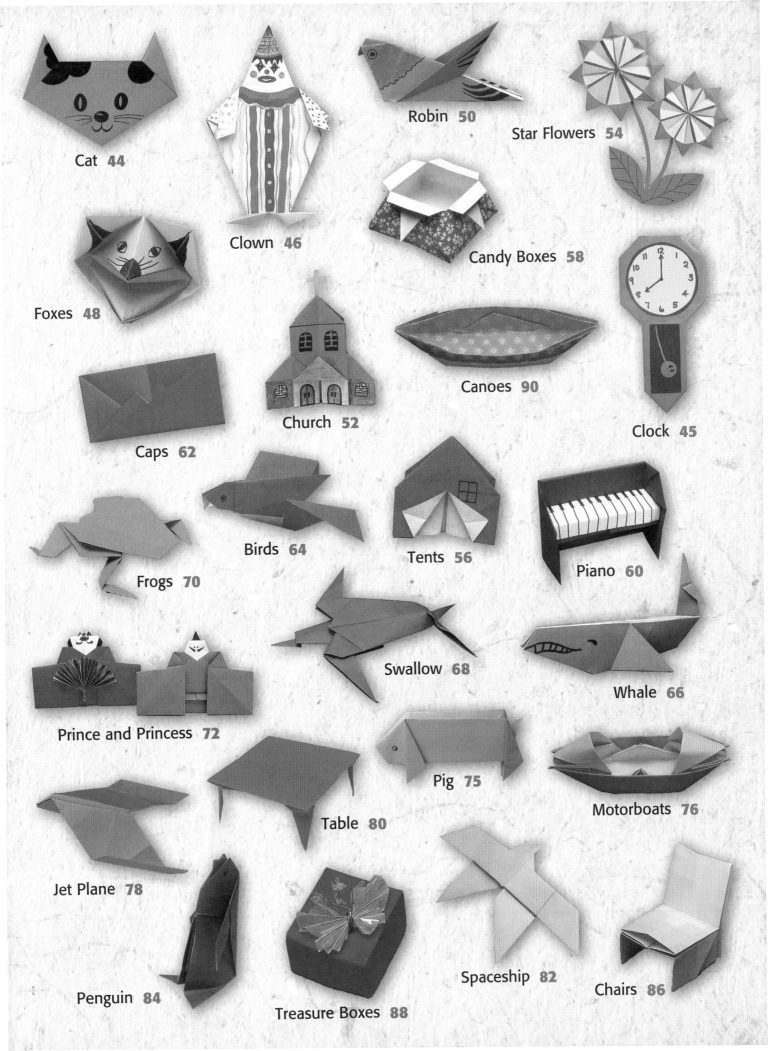

Foreword

Back in 1977 when I was seven years old, I was looking to get my hands on what would be my very first origami book. I convinced my parents to get me the *Origami* series by Florence Sakade. To this day I still find the metamorphosis of the motorboat to be magical, the underlying geometry of the cup to be fascinating and the crane to be the quintessential icon of origami.

More than four decades later, the folks at Tuttle Publishing presented me with the opportunity to revise this now classic book. I was pleasantly surprised at how my own origami journey had come full circle with this chance to spruce up this collection for a new generation of folders. Back when Sakade originally compiled these origami pieces in 1957, her source material consisted largely of sparsely-illustrated notes that were published in difficult-to-find books. It was an impressive and important undertaking to get these traditional paper folds into the mainstream. I feel honored to help keep this book alive, and it is my wish that you will find these ageless works to be as inspiring as they were to me.

— Marc Kirschenbaum

Introduction

Origami, the stimulating hobby of paper folding, has a long tradition in Japan. For more than ten centuries, it has been a favorite pastime with Japanese children, and continues to occupy an important place in their lives. Even very young Japanese children can create intricate figures through step-by-step foldings of square pieces of colored paper. Some become so skilled that they can fold an object such as a bird from a one-inch square of paper or a candy wrapper. Origami objects are regularly used to decorate gifts, adorn bulletin boards in classrooms and grace storefront displays.

Fascination with origami has spread throughout the world. While children enjoy origami as a pleasurable pastime, parents and teachers value it for its educational merits. The ability to follow directions, for example, is an invaluable skill. Moreover, folding origami calls for patience, accuracy and concentrated attention. Because children must also select suitable colors for projects from among those available, they develop an awareness of aesthetics. Japanese paper folding thus offers not only hours of peaceful recreation and the pleasure of accomplishment when a solid figure has been made from a little piece of paper, but it also improves the mental acuity and manual dexterity of those who enjoy it.

Even beginners can fold the objects in this book with a little practice. The step-by-step diagrams and accompanying instructions are extremely easy to follow. The most difficult object to make in the book is the Crane—but it is also the most fun!

Here are some tips for those who are just beginning to try their hand at origami:

1. All of the objects illustrated in this book are made by folding perfectly square pieces of paper. At first, five- or six-inch squares are the easiest to work with. Use thin paper—not heavy construction paper or art paper.
2. You must carefully follow the directions in sequence. Proper shapes can only be obtained through accurate folding.
3. If the diagrams seem too complicated, practice first by inscribing your folding paper with marks that correspond to those in the diagrams.
4. It is a good idea to practice making an object with ordinary paper first, so as not to waste your colorful paper.
5. For a delightful multi-color effect, use two sheets of different colors placed back to back and fold them simultaneously, or adhere them together before folding using spray adhesive. "Duo" origami paper, which has a different color on each side, is an elegant—and thinner—alternative.

— Florence Sakade

Symbols and Terminology

Valley Fold

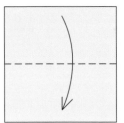 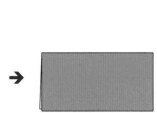

Valley fold in half. **The completed valley fold.**

A dashed line with an open-headed arrow indicates a valley fold (fold forward in the direction of the arrow).

Mountain Fold

Mountain fold in half. **The completed mountain fold.**

A dashed line with dots along with a closed-headed arrow indicates a mountain fold (fold behind in the direction of the arrow).

Precrease

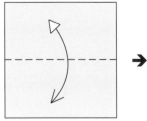 

Precrease in half. **The completed precrease.**

A valley fold line with a double-headed arrow indicates a precrease (valley fold, and then unfold in the direction of the open headed arrow). The resulting crease is represented by a thin line.

Turn Over

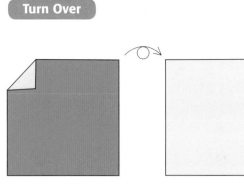

A looped arrow indicates that you should turn the paper over.

Hidden/Imaginary Lines

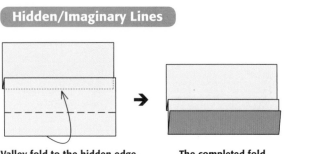

Valley fold to the hidden edge. **The completed fold.**

Hidden/imaginary lines are indicated by a thin dotted line.

Inside-Reverse Fold

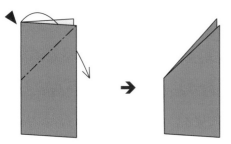

Inside-reverse fold the corner. **The completed inside-reverse fold.**

A solid arrow indicates that you should push in or invert the paper at the indicated area for an inside-reverse fold or for a squash fold (see below).

Squash Fold

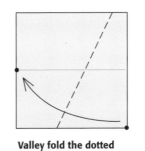

Squash fold the corner. **The completed squash fold.**

Pivot the paper along the indicated lines, and then squash it flat.

Landmark Dots

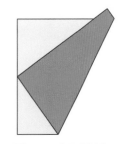

Valley fold the dotted corner to the dotted crease. **The completed fold.**

Dots are sometimes used to call attention to specific landmarks.

Cut the Paper

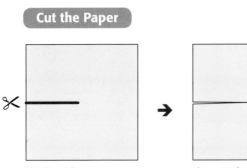

Cut the side. **The completed cut.**

A heavy line with a scissors icon indicates that you should make a cut along that line.

Divided Bracket

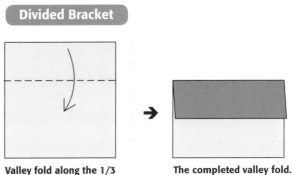

Valley fold along the 1/3 mark. **The completed valley fold.**

A divided bracket with tick marks shows equal divisions.

Dolls

Dolls are an important part of Japanese culture, and the Hinamatsuri celebration showcases royal figurines in classical garb. Follow the suggested coloring patterns to make these paper renditions exhibit a traditional look.

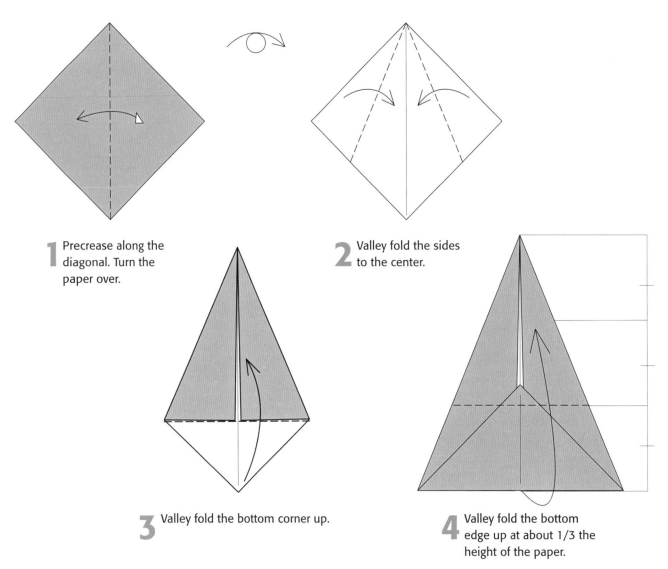

1 Precrease along the diagonal. Turn the paper over.

2 Valley fold the sides to the center.

3 Valley fold the bottom corner up.

4 Valley fold the bottom edge up at about 1/3 the height of the paper.

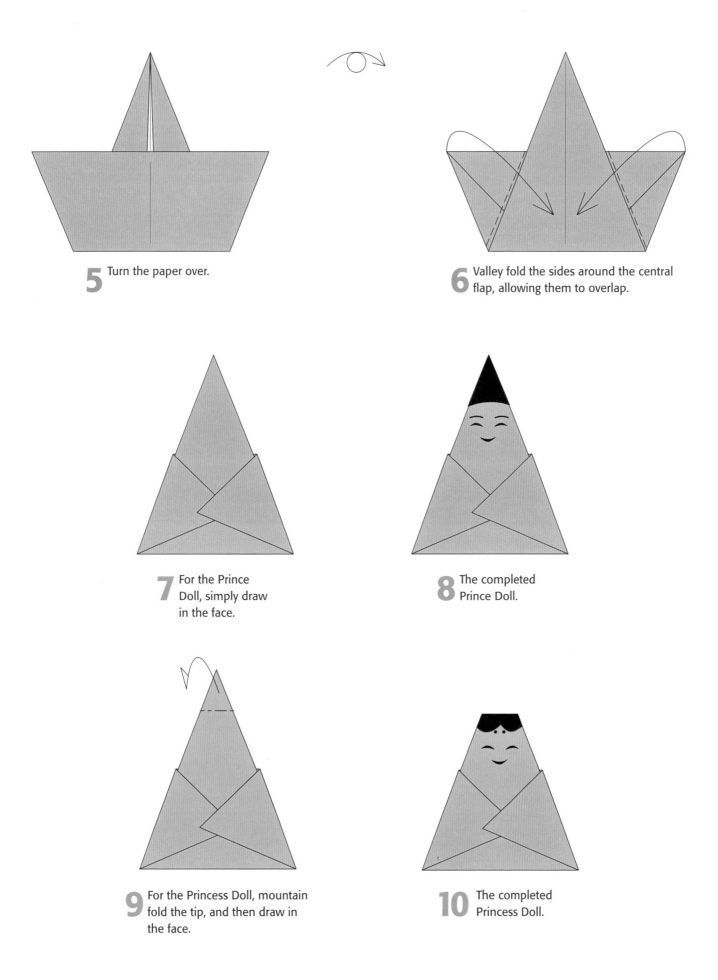

5 Turn the paper over.

6 Valley fold the sides around the central flap, allowing them to overlap.

7 For the Prince Doll, simply draw in the face.

8 The completed Prince Doll.

9 For the Princess Doll, mountain fold the tip, and then draw in the face.

10 The completed Princess Doll.

Fans

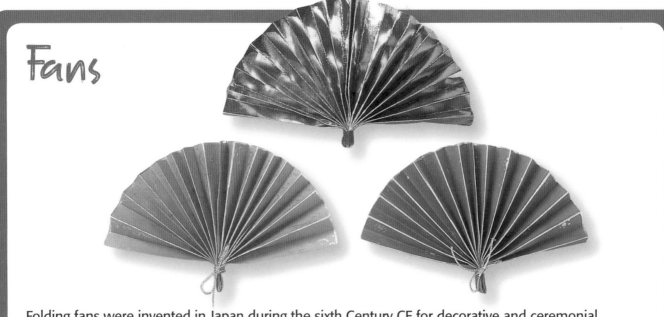

Folding fans were invented in Japan during the sixth Century CE for decorative and ceremonial purposes. They were used to convey a high social status through their lavish ornamentation. Likewise, you can have fun decorating your paper fan, and even use nice wrapping papers to make them.

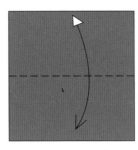

1 Precrease in half.

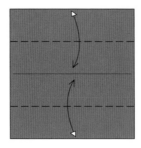

2 Precrease the top and bottom sections in half.

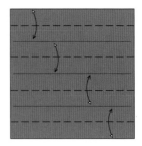

3 Form additional precreases between each section.

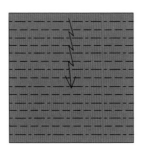

4 Pleat the paper by adding a mountain fold in-between each existing valley crease.

5 Pull the pleats toward each other and secure both halves of the top edge together with a little glue.

6 Pinch the base of the fan together and secure it with a piece of string or yarn.

7 The completed Fan.

Sailboats

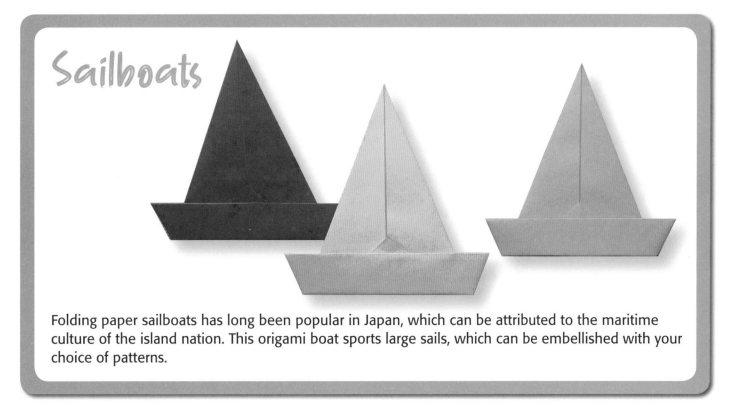

Folding paper sailboats has long been popular in Japan, which can be attributed to the maritime culture of the island nation. This origami boat sports large sails, which can be embellished with your choice of patterns.

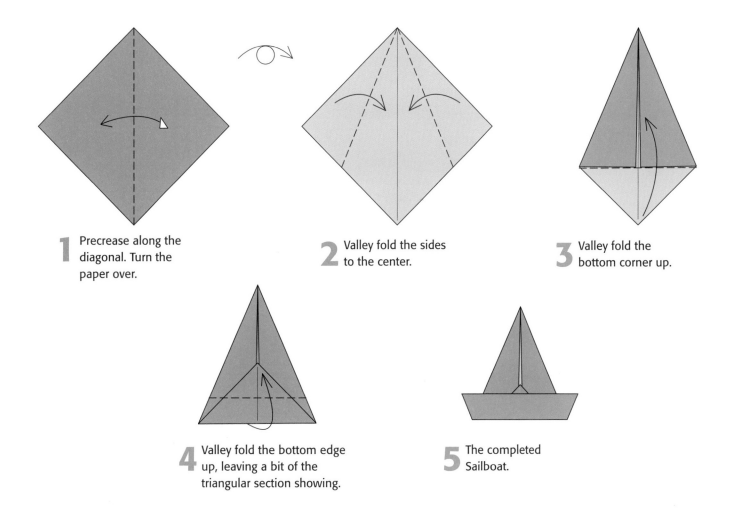

1 Precrease along the diagonal. Turn the paper over.

2 Valley fold the sides to the center.

3 Valley fold the bottom corner up.

4 Valley fold the bottom edge up, leaving a bit of the triangular section showing.

5 The completed Sailboat.

Santa Claus

Santa Claus is famous for handling the incredible task of ensuring that boys and girls around the world get their Christmas gifts. He does get a bit of help from postal workers who guarantee that letters with wish lists get to him. This paper rendition is flat, so it will work well as part of a holiday card or decoration.

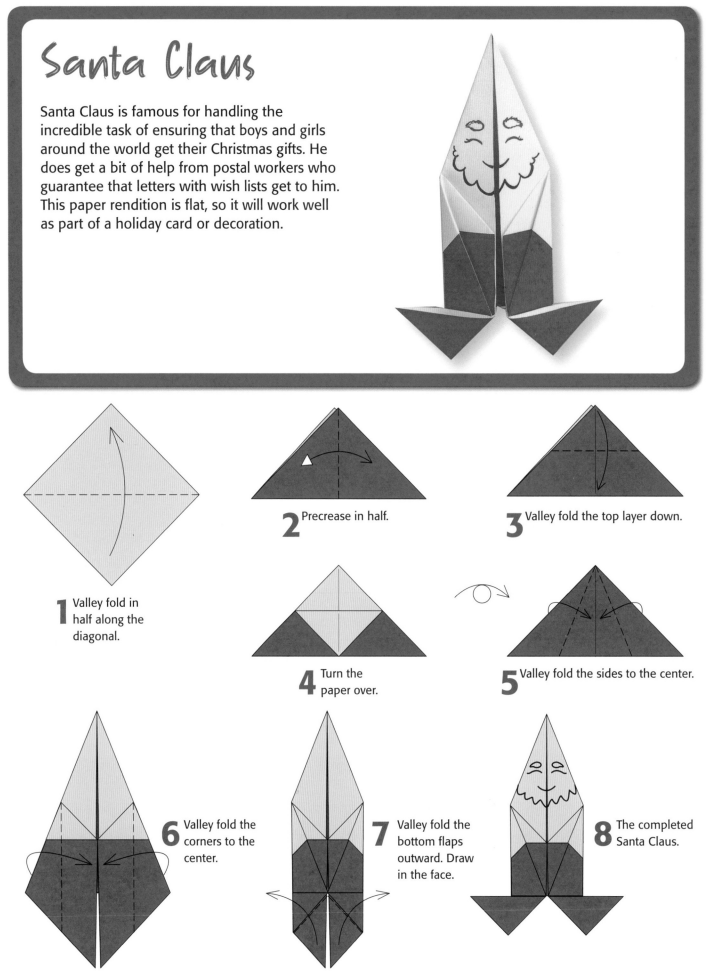

1 Valley fold in half along the diagonal.

2 Precrease in half.

3 Valley fold the top layer down.

4 Turn the paper over.

5 Valley fold the sides to the center.

6 Valley fold the corners to the center.

7 Valley fold the bottom flaps outward. Draw in the face.

8 The completed Santa Claus.

Cups

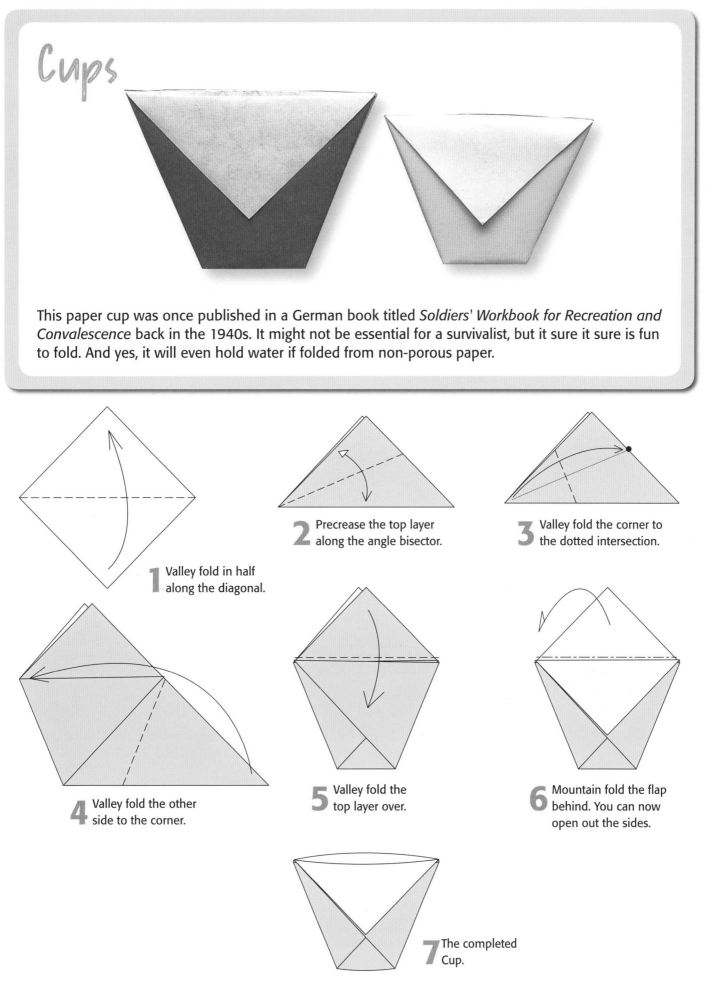

This paper cup was once published in a German book titled *Soldiers' Workbook for Recreation and Convalescence* back in the 1940s. It might not be essential for a survivalist, but it sure it sure is fun to fold. And yes, it will even hold water if folded from non-porous paper.

1 Valley fold in half along the diagonal.

2 Precrease the top layer along the angle bisector.

3 Valley fold the corner to the dotted intersection.

4 Valley fold the other side to the corner.

5 Valley fold the top layer over.

6 Mountain fold the flap behind. You can now open out the sides.

7 The completed Cup.

Christmas Trees

This paper tree is purposefully left simple to be a blank canvas for your holiday decorations. You can fold it large so you can glue on other origami pieces as ornaments (or fold your ornaments in miniature). Of course, using colored pens and shiny papers can make a strong statement too.

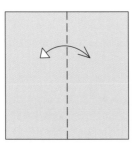

1 Precrease in half.

2 Valley fold the sides to the center.

3 Precrease the corner.

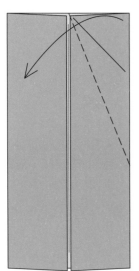

4 Valley fold the corner so that the crease from step 3 lies along the center.

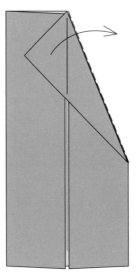

5 Unfold the flap.

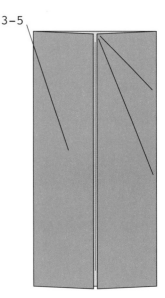

6 Repeat steps 3–5 in mirror image.

14

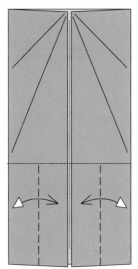

7 Precrease the sides in half. Avoid folding beyond the imaginary line.

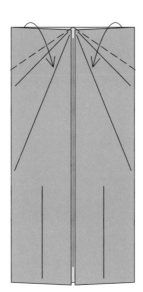

8 Valley fold the corners to lie along the innermost set of creases.

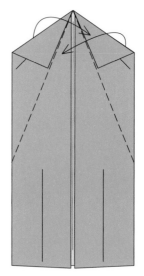

9 Valley fold the sides along the existing creases, allowing them to overlap.

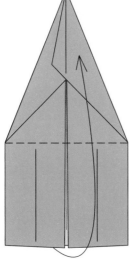

10 Valley fold the bottom flap up.

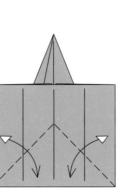

11 Precrease the corners along the angle bisectors.

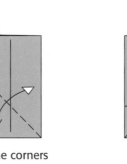

12 Valley fold the flap down through the dotted intersection of creases.

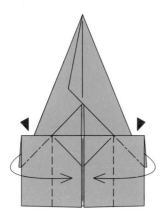

13 Valley fold the sides to the center, squash folding the corners flat.

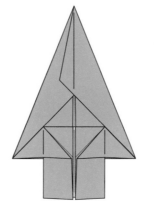

14 Turn the paper over. Decorate the tree using colored pens or shiny papers.

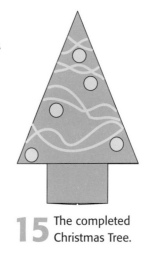

15 The completed Christmas Tree.

Flowers

Flowers come in a wide variety of shapes, and this paper version has a flexible structure that can accommodate the look of many of them. Varying the cutting pattern used accomplishes this. You can experiment and make up your own outline to cut along—imaginary flowers can be fun too!

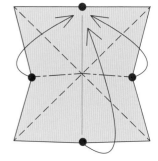

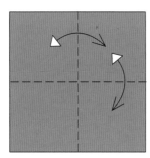

1 Precrease the sides in half. Turn the paper over.

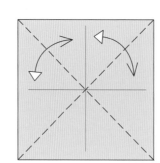

2 Precrease along the diagonals.

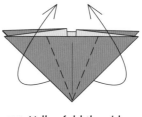

3 Bring the dotted points together using the existing creases.

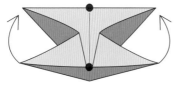

4 Step 3 in progress. Flatten the model.

5 Valley fold the side flaps up to the top.

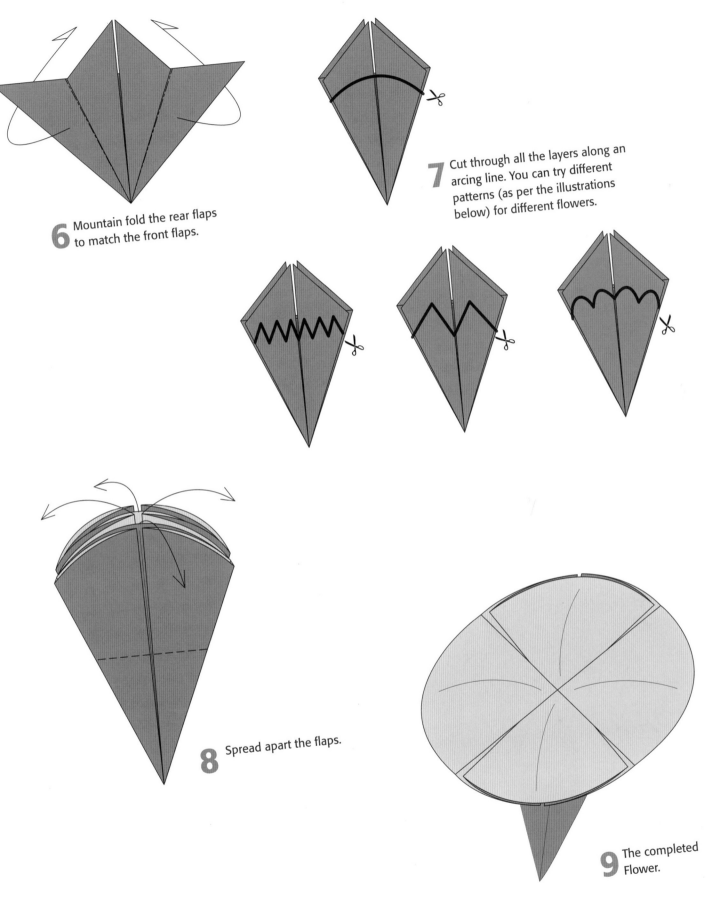

6 Mountain fold the rear flaps to match the front flaps.

7 Cut through all the layers along an arcing line. You can try different patterns (as per the illustrations below) for different flowers.

8 Spread apart the flaps.

9 The completed Flower.

Samurai Helmets

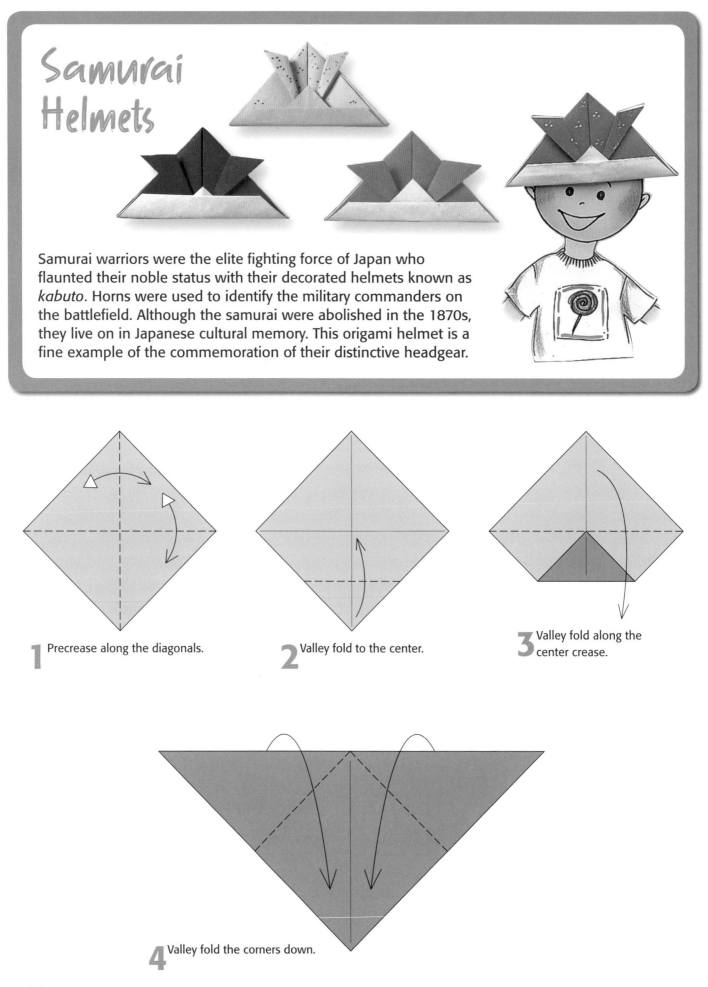

Samurai warriors were the elite fighting force of Japan who flaunted their noble status with their decorated helmets known as *kabuto*. Horns were used to identify the military commanders on the battlefield. Although the samurai were abolished in the 1870s, they live on in Japanese cultural memory. This origami helmet is a fine example of the commemoration of their distinctive headgear.

1 Precrease along the diagonals.

2 Valley fold to the center.

3 Valley fold along the center crease.

4 Valley fold the corners down.

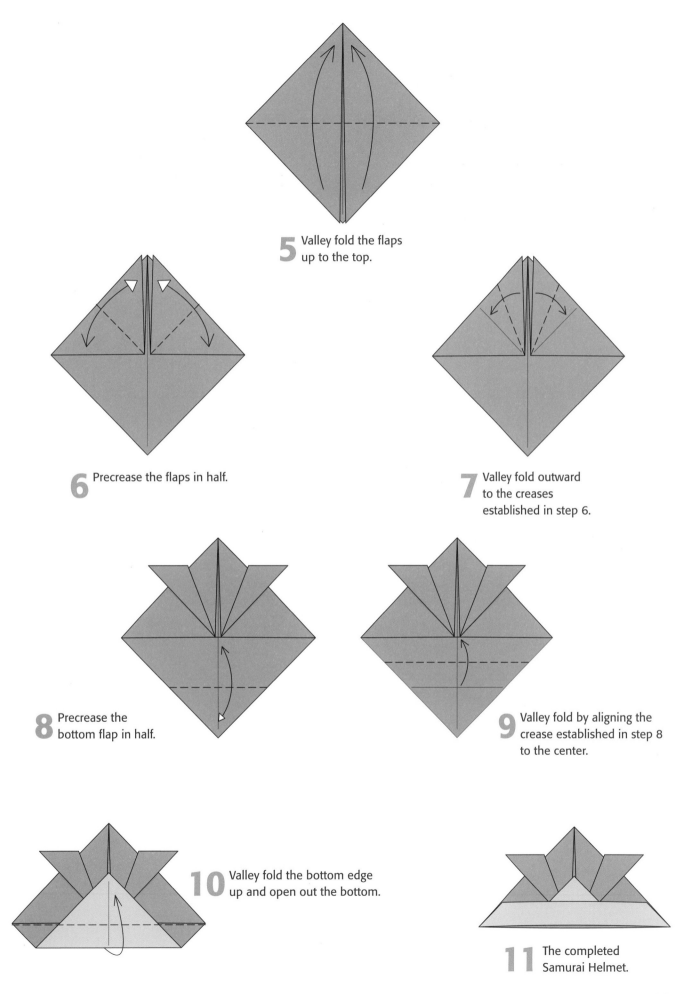

5 Valley fold the flaps up to the top.

6 Precrease the flaps in half.

7 Valley fold outward to the creases established in step 6.

8 Precrease the bottom flap in half.

9 Valley fold by aligning the crease established in step 8 to the center.

10 Valley fold the bottom edge up and open out the bottom.

11 The completed Samurai Helmet.

Ships

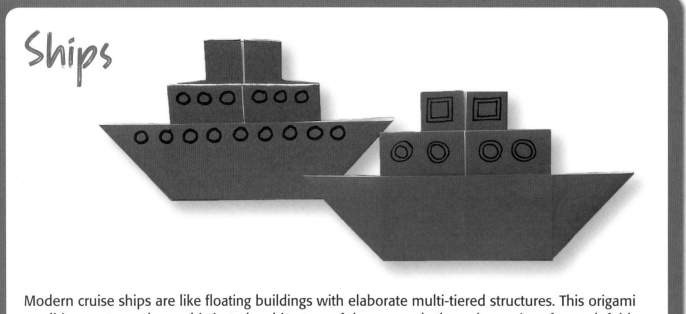

Modern cruise ships are like floating buildings with elaborate multi-tiered structures. This origami rendition captures the sophisticated architecture of these vessels through a series of squash folds that cause each successive level to become narrower.

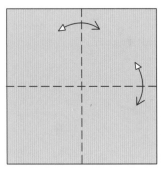

1 Precrease the sides in half.

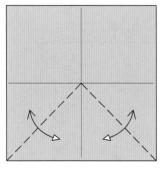

2 Precrease along the lower diagonals.

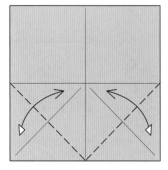

3 Valley fold the bottom corners to the center, and then unfold them.

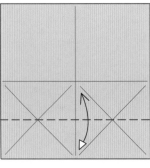

4 Valley fold the bottom edge to the center, and then unfold.

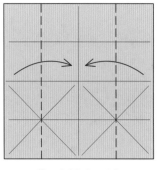

5 Valley fold the sides to the center.

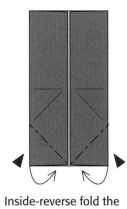

6 Inside-reverse fold the bottom corners.

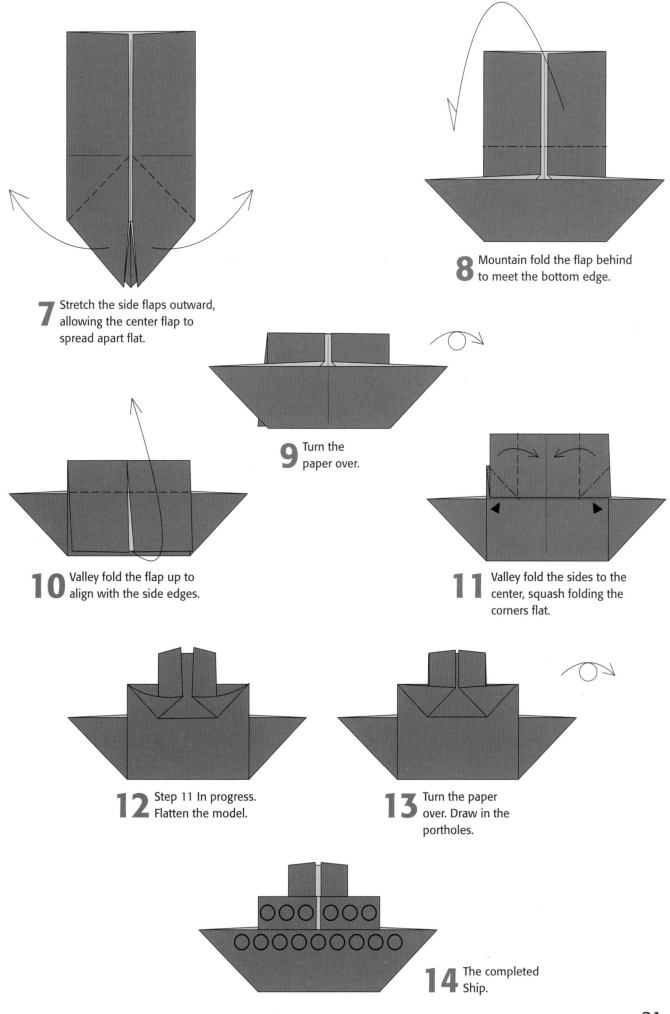

7 Stretch the side flaps outward, allowing the center flap to spread apart flat.

8 Mountain fold the flap behind to meet the bottom edge.

9 Turn the paper over.

10 Valley fold the flap up to align with the side edges.

11 Valley fold the sides to the center, squash folding the corners flat.

12 Step 11 In progress. Flatten the model.

13 Turn the paper over. Draw in the portholes.

14 The completed Ship.

Lanterns

Lanterns were created to be a portable source of illumination, and in Japan they hold special significance because they are part of the traditional tea ceremony. These lamps came to represent love, brightness and protection from evil. You can safely bring some of this warmth into your home with this origami rendition.

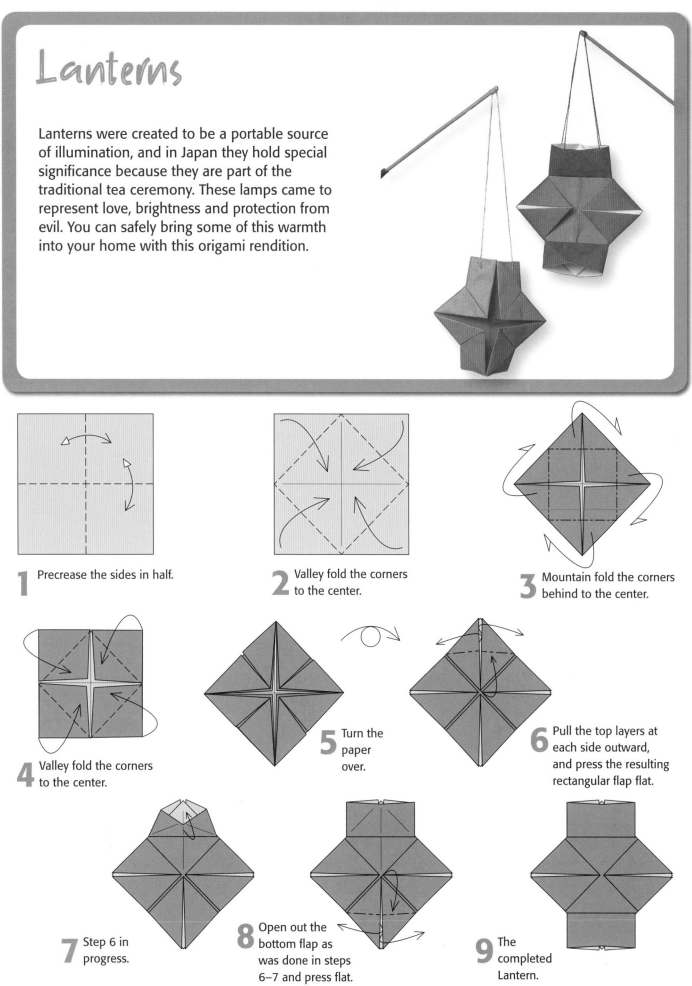

1 Precrease the sides in half.

2 Valley fold the corners to the center.

3 Mountain fold the corners behind to the center.

4 Valley fold the corners to the center.

5 Turn the paper over.

6 Pull the top layers at each side outward, and press the resulting rectangular flap flat.

7 Step 6 in progress.

8 Open out the bottom flap as was done in steps 6–7 and press flat.

9 The completed Lantern.

22

Fish

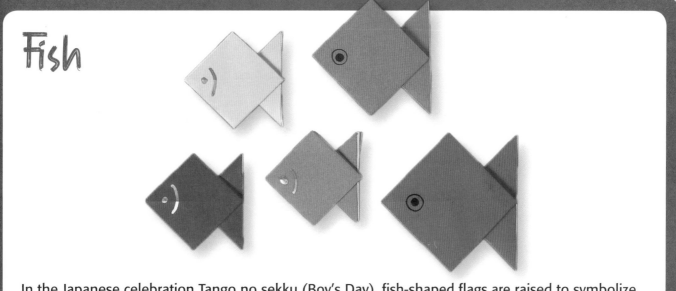

In the Japanese celebration Tango no sekku (Boy's Day), fish-shaped flags are raised to symbolize the metamorphosis of carp to the powerful dragon. Origami fish have come to be known as symbols of peace and happiness. They are also used as gifts for teachers and students, because a group of fish is known as a school.

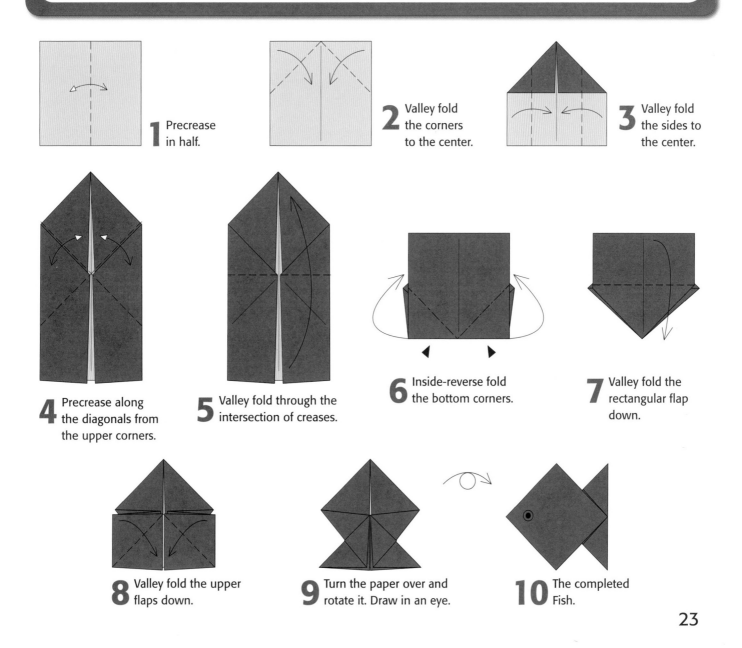

1 Precrease in half.

2 Valley fold the corners to the center.

3 Valley fold the sides to the center.

4 Precrease along the diagonals from the upper corners.

5 Valley fold through the intersection of creases.

6 Inside-reverse fold the bottom corners.

7 Valley fold the rectangular flap down.

8 Valley fold the upper flaps down.

9 Turn the paper over and rotate it. Draw in an eye.

10 The completed Fish.

Windmill

Not all classic origami hails from the East—there is a rich tradition of paper folding in Europe. This windmill is one of the most famous examples of origami developed in Germany, likely inspired by this model's energy-generating namesake. It was first published in the late 1800s. Tack this model to a straw or pencil and watch it spin in the wind!

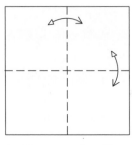

1 Precrease the sides in half.

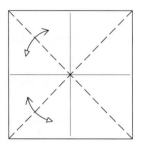

2 Precrease along the diagonals.

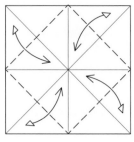

3 Valley fold the corners to the center, and then unfold them.

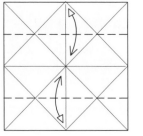

4 Valley fold the sides to the center, and then unfold them.

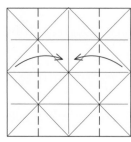

5 Valley fold the sides to the center.

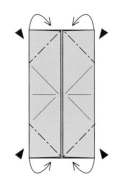

6 Inside-reverse fold the four corners.

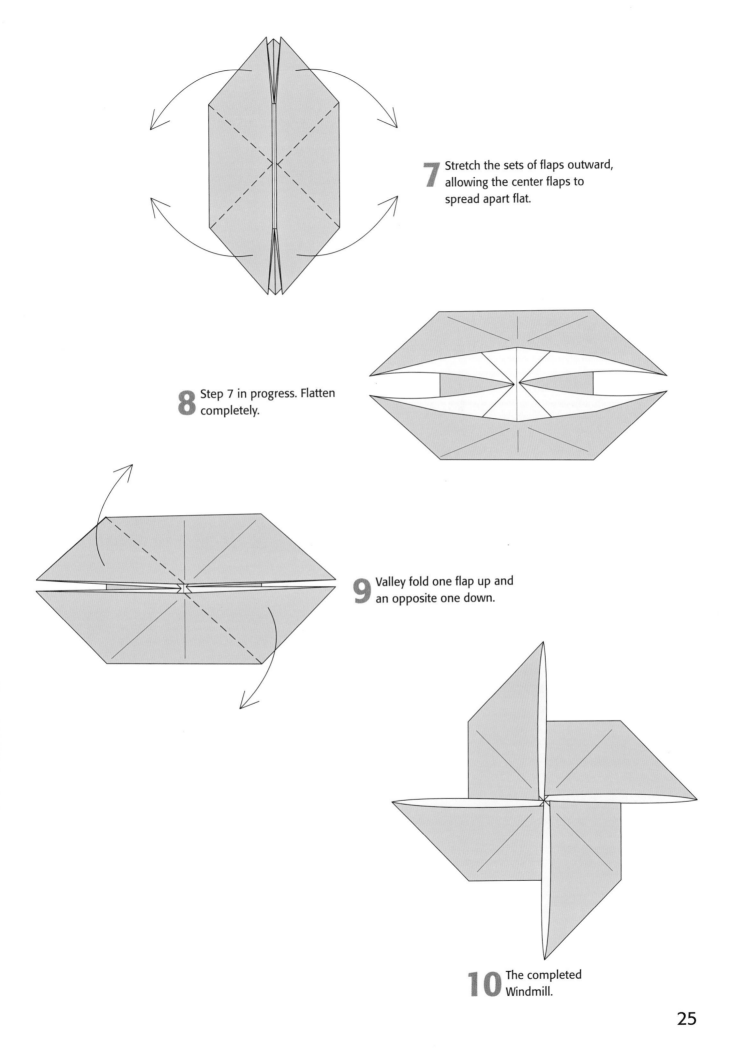

7 Stretch the sets of flaps outward, allowing the center flaps to spread apart flat.

8 Step 7 in progress. Flatten completely.

9 Valley fold one flap up and an opposite one down.

10 The completed Windmill.

Swans

Swans are unusual in the world of animals as they are completely devoted to their mates—until death do they part. This commitment has made this noble bird a symbol of eternal love. You can use this origami swan as a wedding or anniversary decoration.

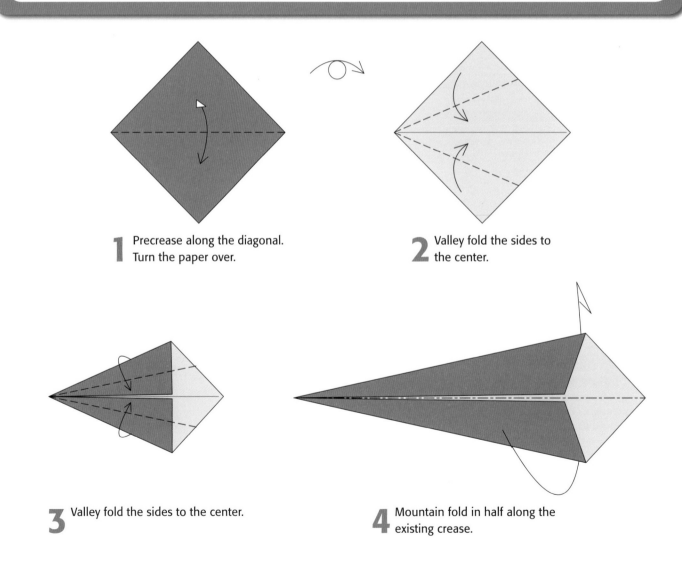

1 Precrease along the diagonal. Turn the paper over.

2 Valley fold the sides to the center.

3 Valley fold the sides to the center.

4 Mountain fold in half along the existing crease.

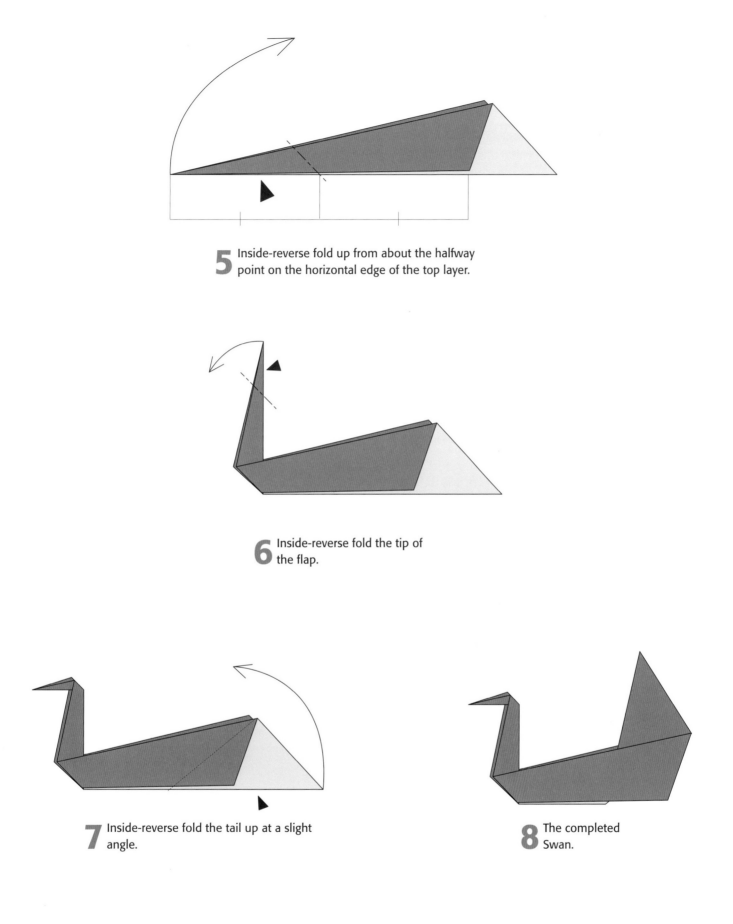

5 Inside-reverse fold up from about the halfway point on the horizontal edge of the top layer.

6 Inside-reverse fold the tip of the flap.

7 Inside-reverse fold the tail up at a slight angle.

8 The completed Swan.

Cranes

In Japan, the crane is a symbol of good luck and can be found, in some form or other, practically any place—in the textile designs on women's kimonos, hung from the ceilings of temples and shrines as offerings from the people who go there to pray, or strung on pieces of thread to decorate a room. Japanese folklore has stories of cranes living for 1,000 years, and legend has it that anyone who folds that same number of this traditional origami piece will be granted a wish from the gods. This origami crane gained significance through the story of Hiroshima atomic-bombing survivor Sadako Sasaki. As a young girl, she attempted to fold the requisite number of cranes to be granted her dream of world peace. People around the world honor her vision by folding this classic model.

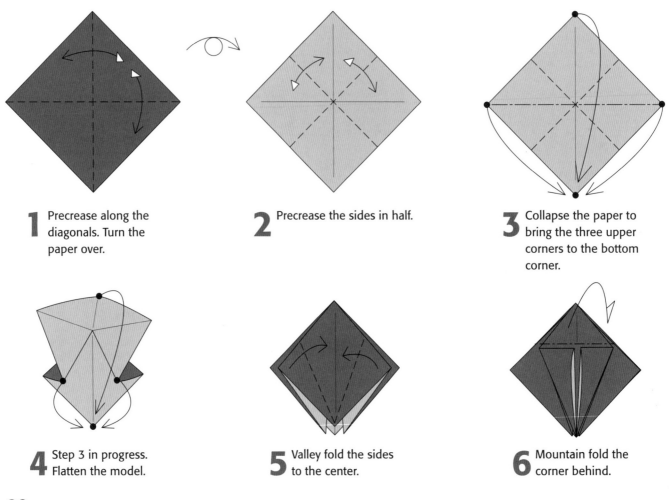

1 Precrease along the diagonals. Turn the paper over.

2 Precrease the sides in half.

3 Collapse the paper to bring the three upper corners to the bottom corner.

4 Step 3 in progress. Flatten the model.

5 Valley fold the sides to the center.

6 Mountain fold the corner behind.

7 Swing the flaps outward.

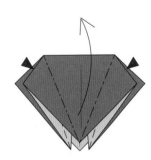

8 Bring the top layer up, allowing the sides to squash fold flat (petal fold).

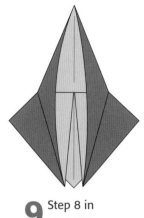

9 Step 8 in progress.

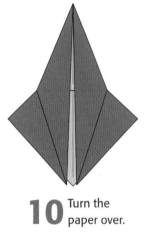

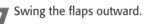

10 Turn the paper over.

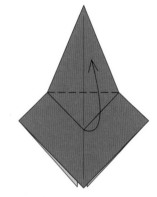

11 Swing the center flap up.

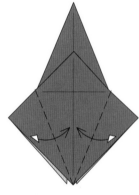

12 Precrease along the angle bisectors.

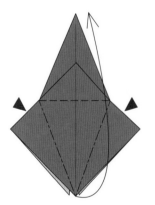

13 Bring the top layer up, allowing the sides to squash fold flat (petal fold).

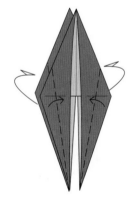

14 Valley fold the sides to the center and repeat behind.

15 Swing over a flap at each side.

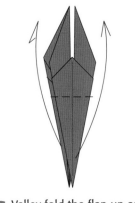

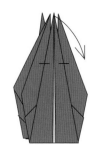

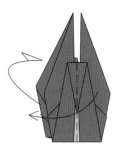

16 Valley fold the flap up as far as possible. Repeat behind.

17 Valley fold the tip of the front flap partway.

18 Swing over a flap at each side.

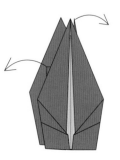

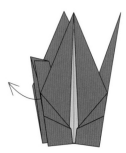

19 Slide out the middle flaps and flatten.

20 Slide the hidden flap up and flatten.

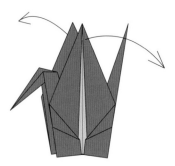

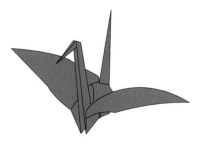

21 Spread apart the wings, allowing the center point to become blunted.

22 The completed Crane.

House

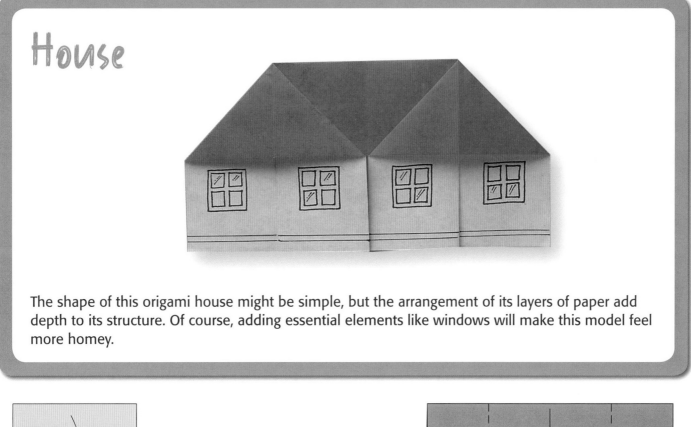

The shape of this origami house might be simple, but the arrangement of its layers of paper add depth to its structure. Of course, adding essential elements like windows will make this model feel more homey.

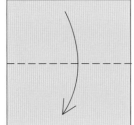

1 Valley fold in half.

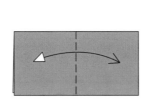

2 Precrease in half.

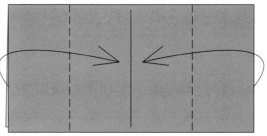

3 Valley fold the sides to the center.

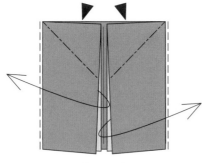

4 Open out the top layers and squash fold the corners. Draw in the windows.

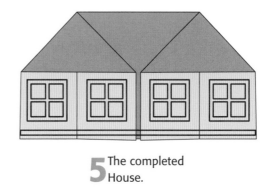

5 The completed House.

Dog

Dogs and humans have enjoyed a companionship that has extended for millennia. Dogs are often regarded as an integral part of the human family. They are also very expressive through the movements of their tails and ears. This origami model depicts a dog's head, with oversized outer flaps serving as floppy ears. You can add even more character through the shape and positioning of the drawn-on eyes and mouth.

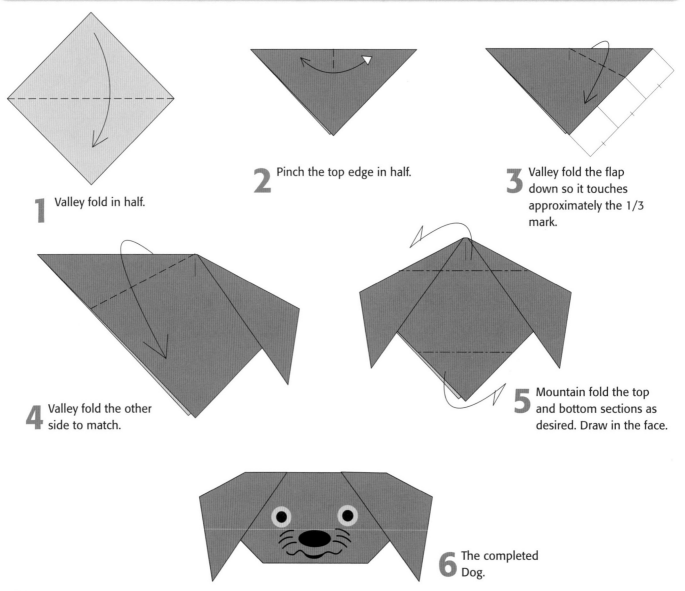

1 Valley fold in half.

2 Pinch the top edge in half.

3 Valley fold the flap down so it touches approximately the 1/3 mark.

4 Valley fold the other side to match.

5 Mountain fold the top and bottom sections as desired. Draw in the face.

6 The completed Dog.

Peacocks

Having a flamboyantly decorated tail is not enough for the male peacock. When they are looking to attract the attention of females, they will also dance around and make loud noises. This origami peacock also has a large tail that you can decorate with bright colors—showy footwork and squawking is optional.

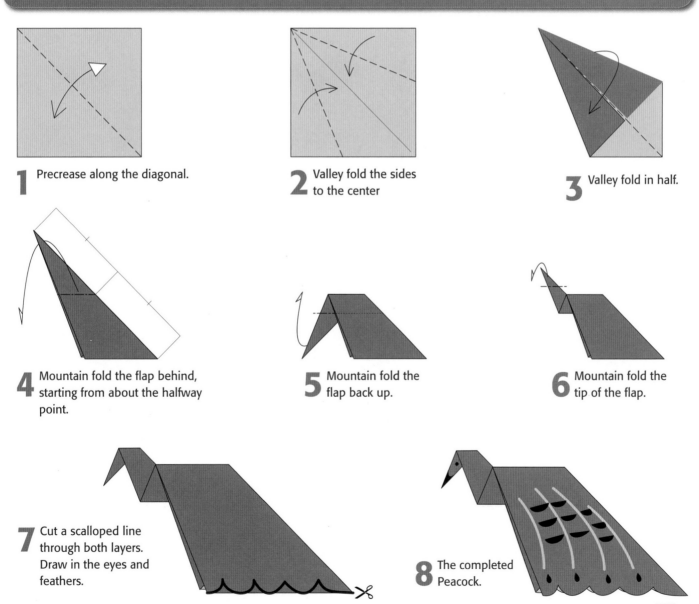

1 Precrease along the diagonal.

2 Valley fold the sides to the center

3 Valley fold in half.

4 Mountain fold the flap behind, starting from about the halfway point.

5 Mountain fold the flap back up.

6 Mountain fold the tip of the flap.

7 Cut a scalloped line through both layers. Draw in the eyes and feathers.

8 The completed Peacock.

33

Wolf

Wolves are highly regarded in Japan, as they were believed to be protectors against the perceived dangers of their mountainous environment. To further protect their villages, wolf charms were fashioned, called *shishiyoke*. If the mythology is true, folding this origami version should give you a comforting feeling of security.

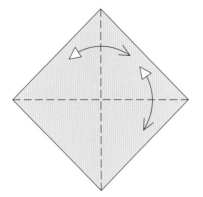

1 Precrease along the diagonals.

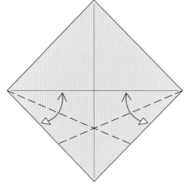

2 Precrease along the angle bisectors.

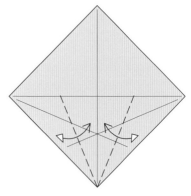

3 Precrease along the angle bisectors. Avoid folding past the middle.

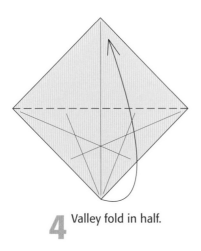

4 Valley fold in half.

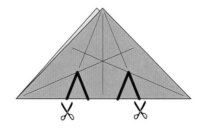

5 Cut out two sections, using the existing creases as guides.

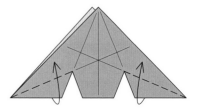

6 Valley fold the bottom edges up.

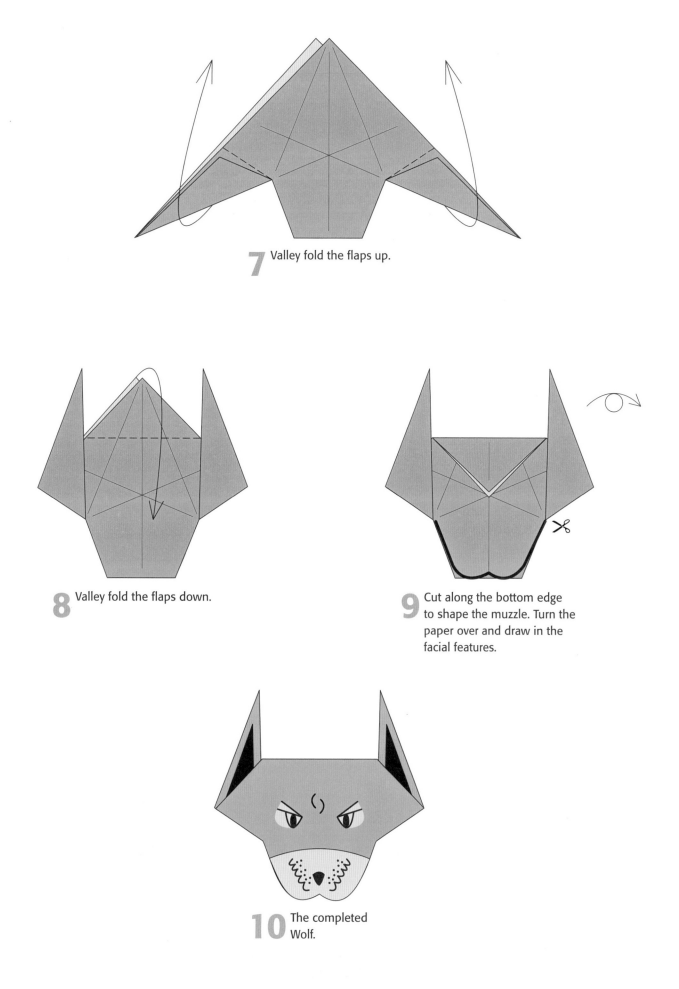

7 Valley fold the flaps up.

8 Valley fold the flaps down.

9 Cut along the bottom edge to shape the muzzle. Turn the paper over and draw in the facial features.

10 The completed Wolf.

Peahen

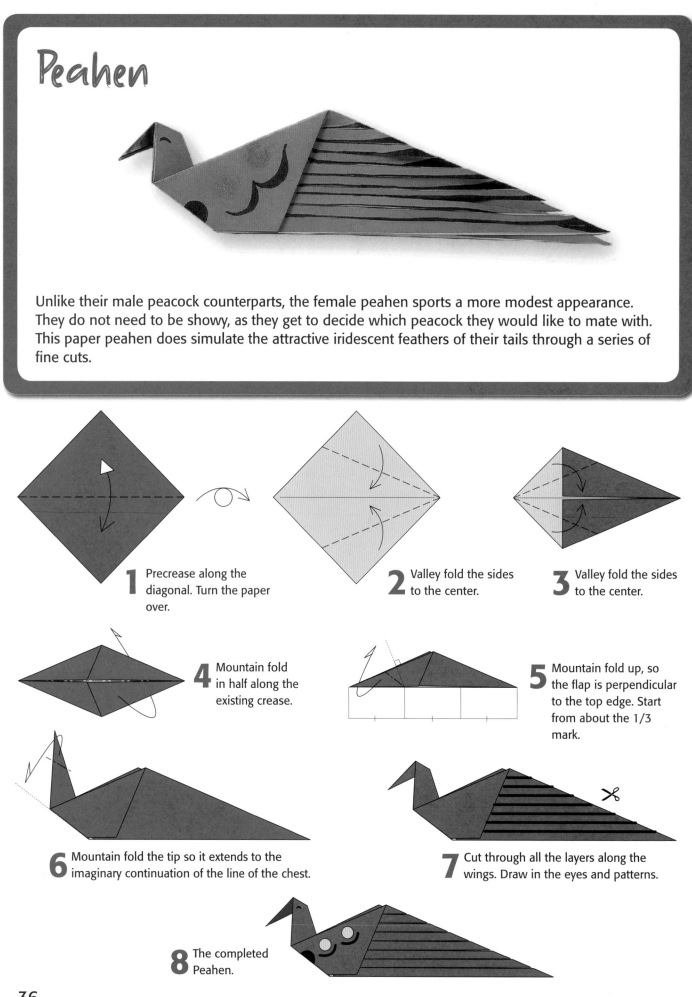

Unlike their male peacock counterparts, the female peahen sports a more modest appearance. They do not need to be showy, as they get to decide which peacock they would like to mate with. This paper peahen does simulate the attractive iridescent feathers of their tails through a series of fine cuts.

1 Precrease along the diagonal. Turn the paper over.

2 Valley fold the sides to the center.

3 Valley fold the sides to the center.

4 Mountain fold in half along the existing crease.

5 Mountain fold up, so the flap is perpendicular to the top edge. Start from about the 1/3 mark.

6 Mountain fold the tip so it extends to the imaginary continuation of the line of the chest.

7 Cut through all the layers along the wings. Draw in the eyes and patterns.

8 The completed Peahen.

Rabbits

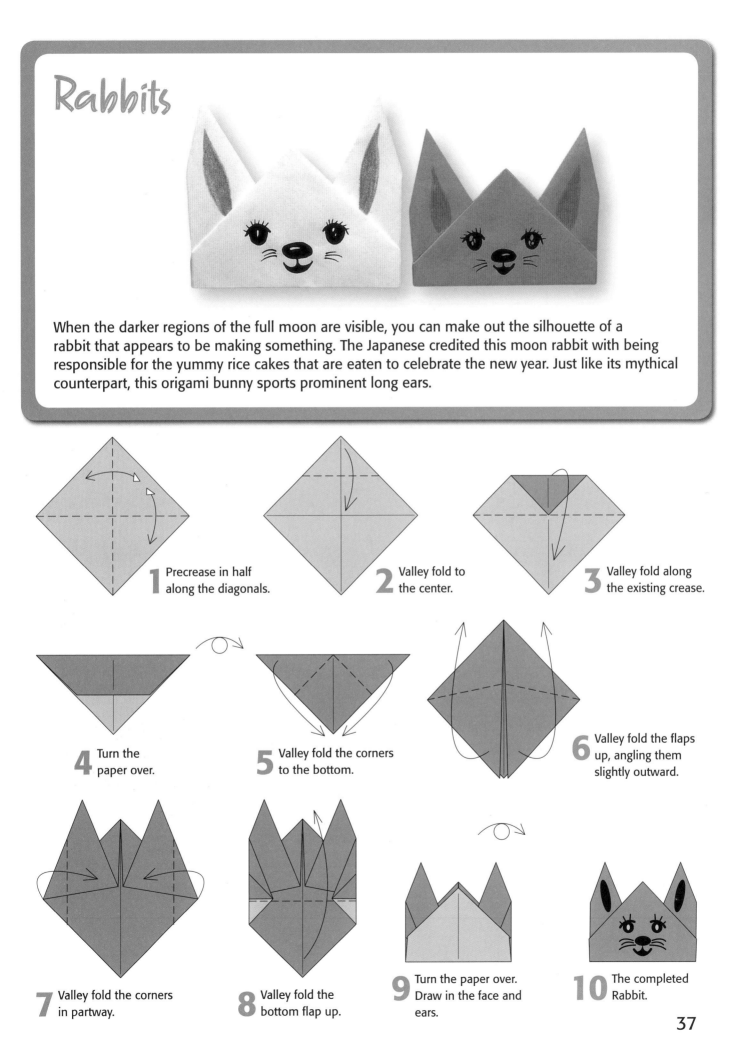

When the darker regions of the full moon are visible, you can make out the silhouette of a rabbit that appears to be making something. The Japanese credited this moon rabbit with being responsible for the yummy rice cakes that are eaten to celebrate the new year. Just like its mythical counterpart, this origami bunny sports prominent long ears.

1 Precrease in half along the diagonals.

2 Valley fold to the center.

3 Valley fold along the existing crease.

4 Turn the paper over.

5 Valley fold the corners to the bottom.

6 Valley fold the flaps up, angling them slightly outward.

7 Valley fold the corners in partway.

8 Valley fold the bottom flap up.

9 Turn the paper over. Draw in the face and ears.

10 The completed Rabbit.

Giraffes

Making an origami giraffe is a tall order with its tricky proportions. This one has shorter legs, so the focus is on the long neck. Adding spots to it will make it unmistakable as the tree-grazing safari animal.

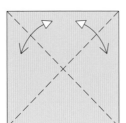

1 Precrease along the diagonals.

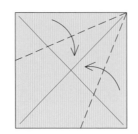

2 Valley fold the sides to the center.

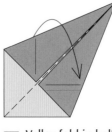

3 Valley fold in half.

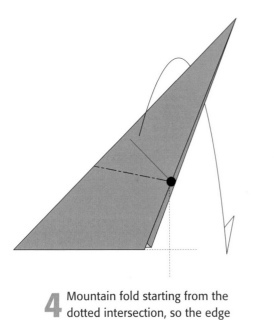

4 Mountain fold starting from the dotted intersection, so the edge is perpendicular to the base.

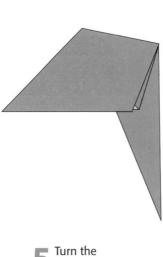

5 Turn the paper over.

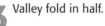

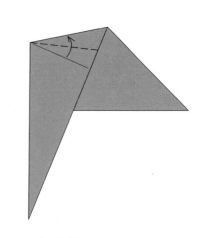

6 Valley fold up so the crease meets the top edge.

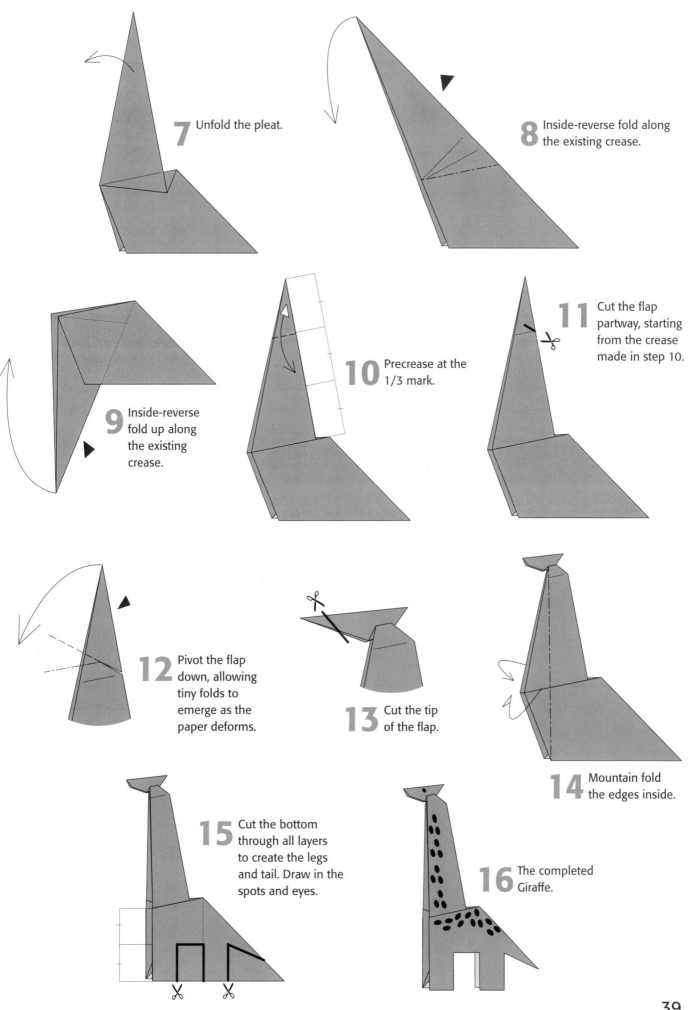

7 Unfold the pleat.

8 Inside-reverse fold along the existing crease.

9 Inside-reverse fold up along the existing crease.

10 Precrease at the 1/3 mark.

11 Cut the flap partway, starting from the crease made in step 10.

12 Pivot the flap down, allowing tiny folds to emerge as the paper deforms.

13 Cut the tip of the flap.

14 Mountain fold the edges inside.

15 Cut the bottom through all layers to create the legs and tail. Draw in the spots and eyes.

16 The completed Giraffe.

Elephant

Sporting an elongated trunk, large ears and a robust body, the elephant is one of the most distinctive-looking animals. This uniqueness has made the large gray animal a favorite subject with origami artists. This one has an exaggerated head with a slight forward slant, so it looks like it is on the move.

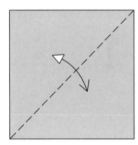

1 Precrease along the diagonal.

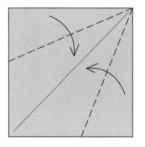

2 Valley fold the sides to the center.

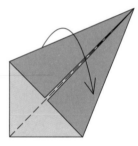

3 Valley fold in half.

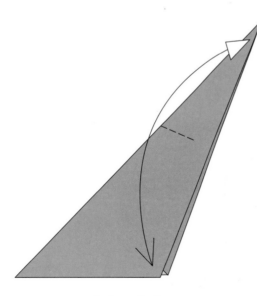

4 Precrease a pinch mark along the edge.

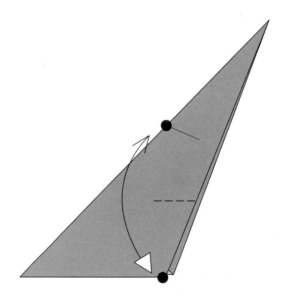

5 Form another pinch mark by bringing the dotted locations together.

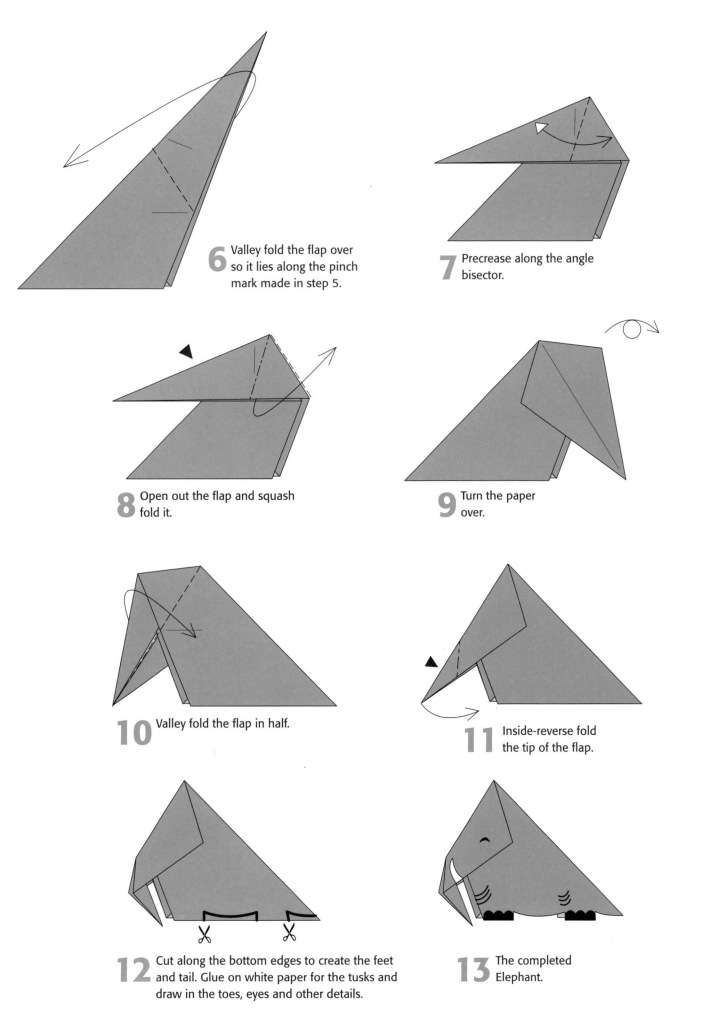

6 Valley fold the flap over so it lies along the pinch mark made in step 5.

7 Precrease along the angle bisector.

8 Open out the flap and squash fold it.

9 Turn the paper over.

10 Valley fold the flap in half.

11 Inside-reverse fold the tip of the flap.

12 Cut along the bottom edges to create the feet and tail. Glue on white paper for the tusks and draw in the toes, eyes and other details.

13 The completed Elephant.

Kimono

Some things never go out of style. The kimono is a rare example of traditional garb that has been continuously worn for centuries in Japan. Unlike most modern apparel, this garment is constructed from a single piece of material. This makes it ideal as a traditional origami subject, which also requires a single piece of paper to be used.

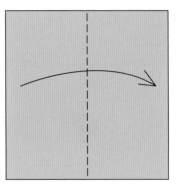

1 Valley fold in half.

2 Lightly pinch the edge in half.

3 Pinch the edge of the upper section in half.

4 Pinch the edge in half again.

5 Mountain fold the top edge to the crease made in step 4.

6 Precrease in half.

7 Valley fold the corners inward, leaving a small gap at the center.

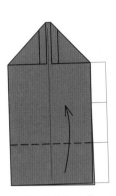

8 Valley fold at about 1/3 the height of the indicated span.

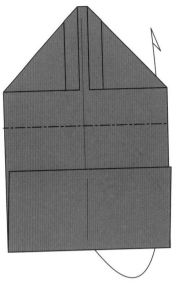

9 Mountain fold midway between the tip of the point and the bottom edge.

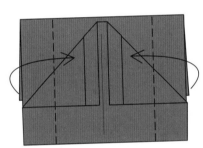

10 Valley fold the edges in to meet the edge of the strip formed in step 5.

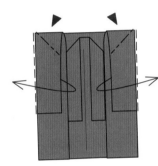

11 Fold the top layers outward, squash folding the top corners.

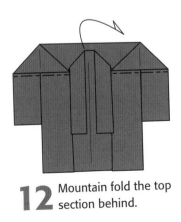

12 Mountain fold the top section behind.

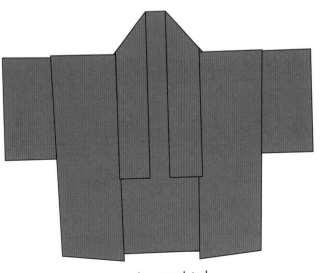

13 The completed Kimono.

Cat

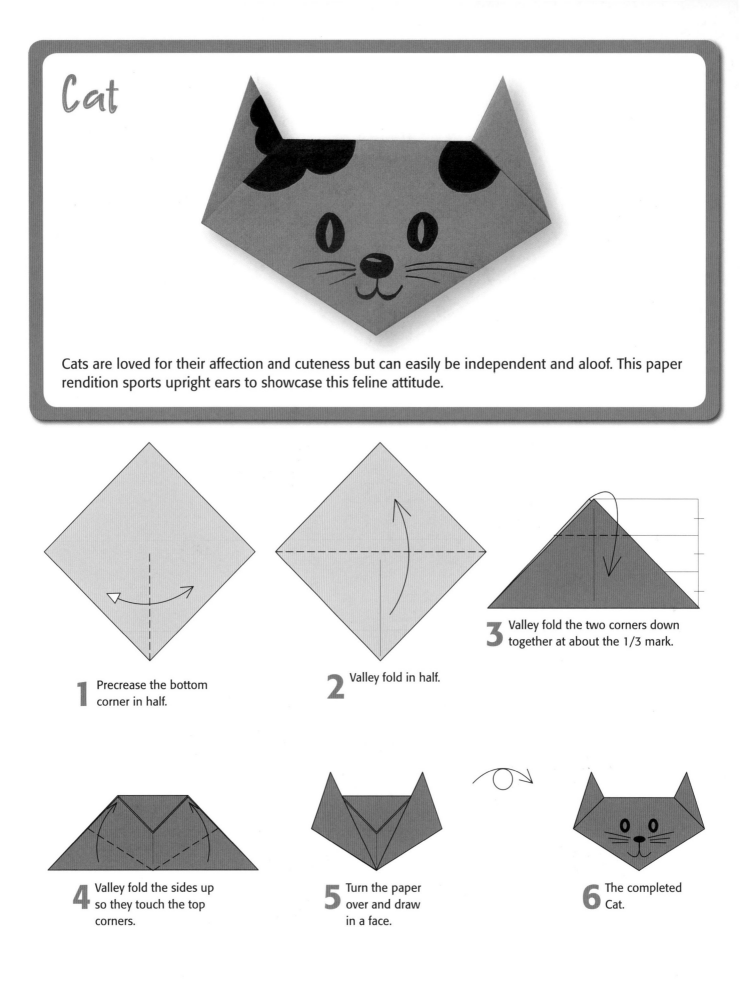

Cats are loved for their affection and cuteness but can easily be independent and aloof. This paper rendition sports upright ears to showcase this feline attitude.

1 Precrease the bottom corner in half.

2 Valley fold in half.

3 Valley fold the two corners down together at about the 1/3 mark.

4 Valley fold the sides up so they touch the top corners.

5 Turn the paper over and draw in a face.

6 The completed Cat.

Clock

When they were first introduced in the 1600s, pendulum-regulated clocks were valued for their accuracy. Although timekeeping technology has improved considerably since then, these handsome structures are still cherished for their rich ornamentation. You can recreate some of that nostalgia through this paper incarnation.

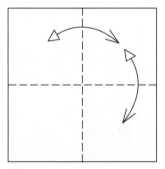

1 Precrease the sides in half.

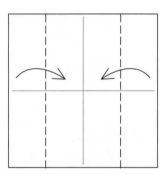

2 Valley fold to the center.

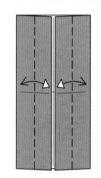

3 Precrease the top single layers in half.

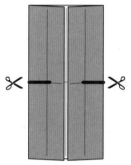

4 Cut the sides up to the creases made in step 3.

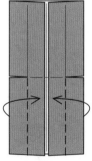

5 Valley fold the bottom section to the center.

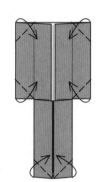

6 Valley fold the corners inward.

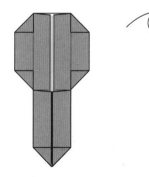

7 Turn the paper over. Glue on a light-colored circle for the face and draw in a dark rectangle background to define the pendulum. Draw in the hands and numbers.

8 The completed Clock.

Clown

Everything about clowns is over the top, from their oversized clothes, makeup that exaggerates their features, and their dramatic movements. This is all done for the sake of entertainment, becoming a parody of what we generally take to be mundane. With this origami clown you can feel comfortable taking the liberty of decorating it as flamboyantly as you wish.

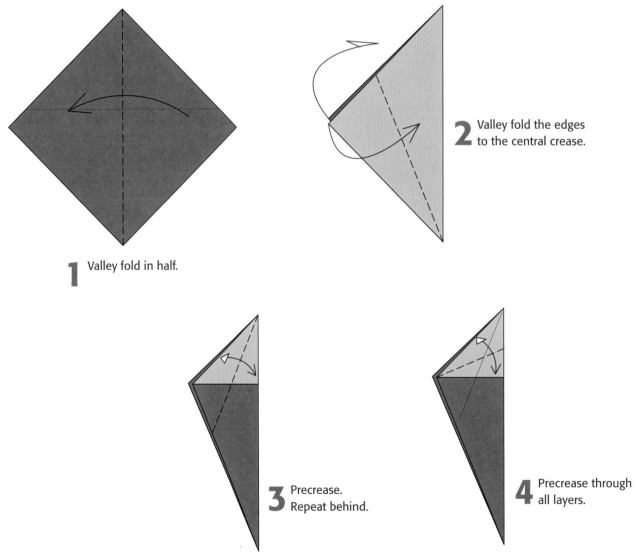

1 Valley fold in half.

2 Valley fold the edges to the central crease.

3 Precrease. Repeat behind.

4 Precrease through all layers.

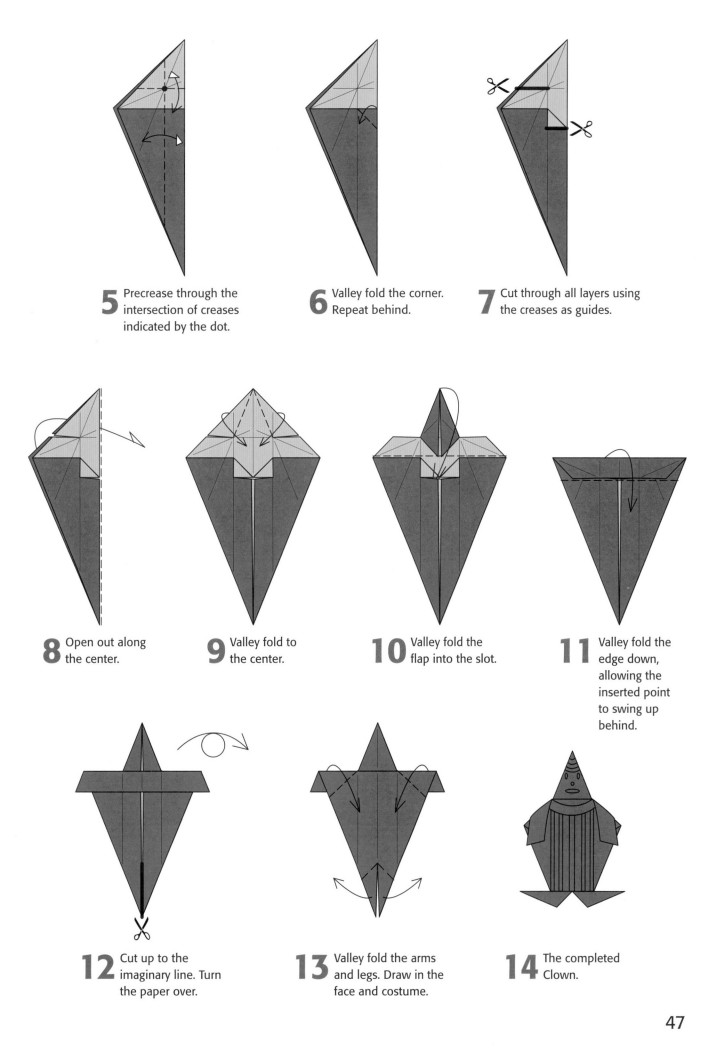

5 Precrease through the intersection of creases indicated by the dot.

6 Valley fold the corner. Repeat behind.

7 Cut through all layers using the creases as guides.

8 Open out along the center.

9 Valley fold to the center.

10 Valley fold the flap into the slot.

11 Valley fold the edge down, allowing the inserted point to swing up behind.

12 Cut up to the imaginary line. Turn the paper over.

13 Valley fold the arms and legs. Draw in the face and costume.

14 The completed Clown.

Foxes

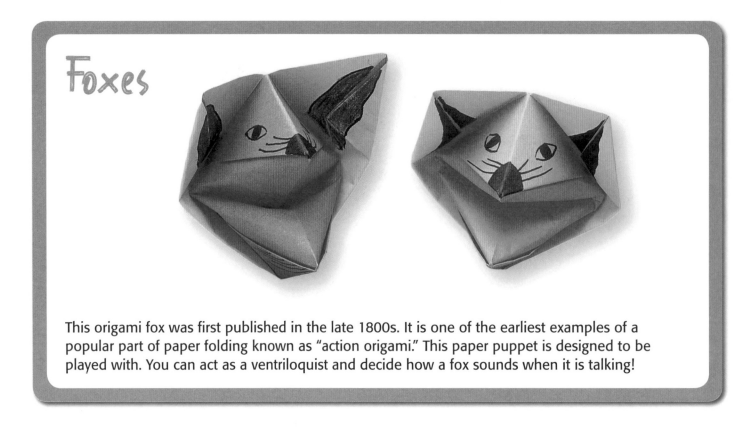

This origami fox was first published in the late 1800s. It is one of the earliest examples of a popular part of paper folding known as "action origami." This paper puppet is designed to be played with. You can act as a ventriloquist and decide how a fox sounds when it is talking!

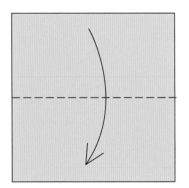

1 Valley fold in half.

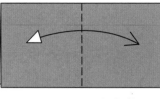

2 Precrease in half.

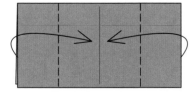

3 Valley fold the sides to the center.

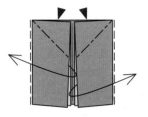

4 Open out the top layers and squash fold the corners.

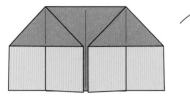

5 Turn the paper over.

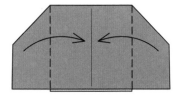

6 Valley fold the sides to the center.

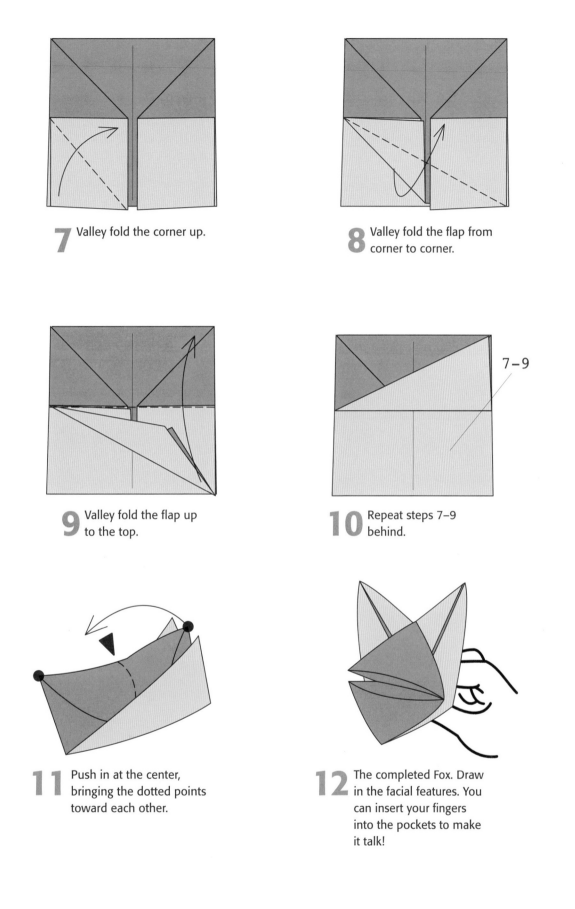

7 Valley fold the corner up.

8 Valley fold the flap from corner to corner.

9 Valley fold the flap up to the top.

10 Repeat steps 7–9 behind.

7–9

11 Push in at the center, bringing the dotted points toward each other.

12 The completed Fox. Draw in the facial features. You can insert your fingers into the pockets to make it talk!

Robin

Some people simply use a calendar to know when spring has arrived, but others will rely on the first appearance of the brightly colored robin as an indicator of the coming of the season. As it turns out, robins are a bit more adaptable to climate changes than we realized. Likewise, you can fold this origami robin any time of the year.

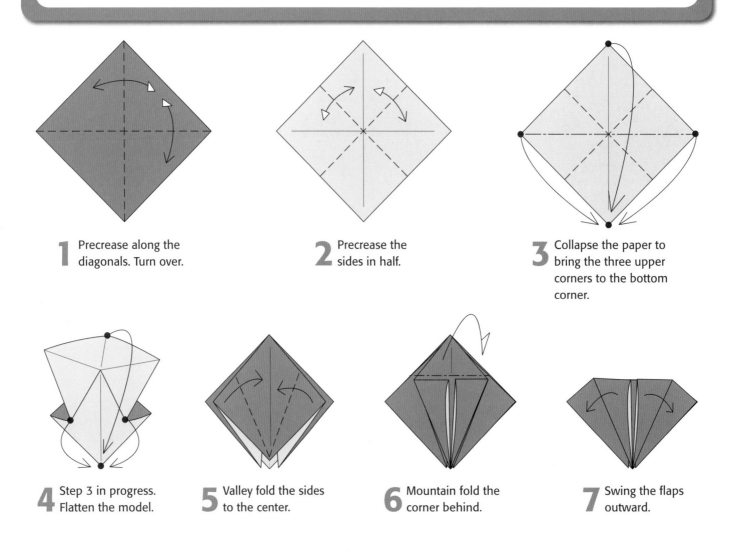

1 Precrease along the diagonals. Turn over.

2 Precrease the sides in half.

3 Collapse the paper to bring the three upper corners to the bottom corner.

4 Step 3 in progress. Flatten the model.

5 Valley fold the sides to the center.

6 Mountain fold the corner behind.

7 Swing the flaps outward.

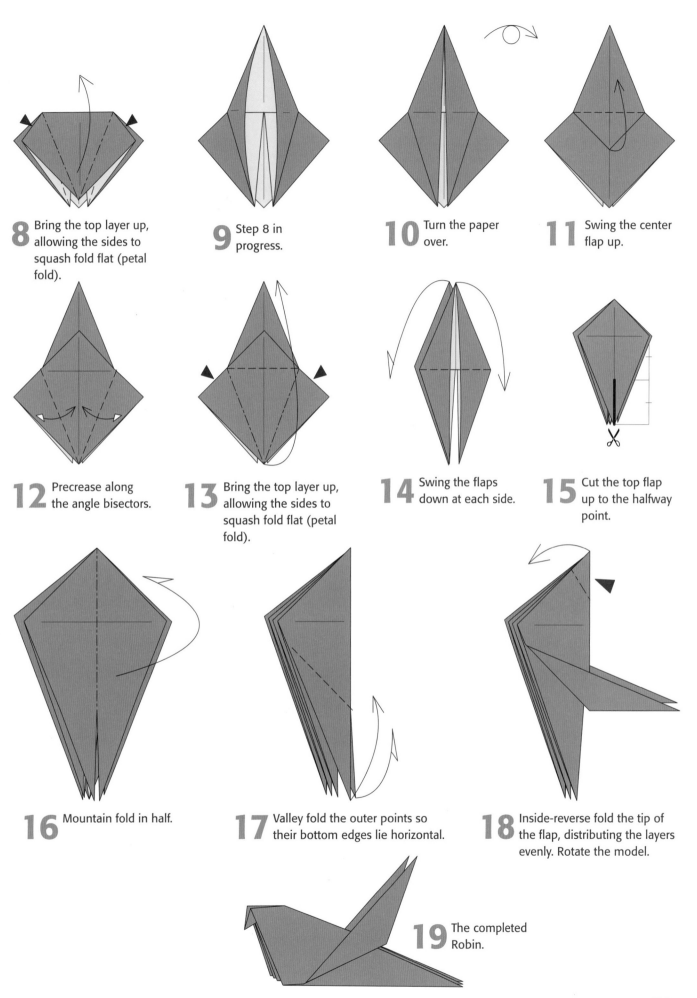

8 Bring the top layer up, allowing the sides to squash fold flat (petal fold).

9 Step 8 in progress.

10 Turn the paper over.

11 Swing the center flap up.

12 Precrease along the angle bisectors.

13 Bring the top layer up, allowing the sides to squash fold flat (petal fold).

14 Swing the flaps down at each side.

15 Cut the top flap up to the halfway point.

16 Mountain fold in half.

17 Valley fold the outer points so their bottom edges lie horizontal.

18 Inside-reverse fold the tip of the flap, distributing the layers evenly. Rotate the model.

19 The completed Robin.

Church

Regardless of religious affiliation, people appreciate the beauty built into church structures, some of which are architectural marvels. Many have become tourist attractions, and models have been built commemorating some of the more famous sites. Design and structure are big parts of origami, so it is fitting to have this paper homage to these houses of worship.

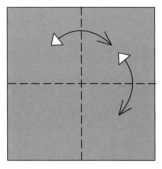

1 Precrease the sides in half. Turn the paper over.

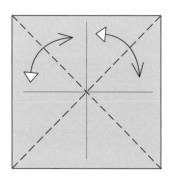

2 Precrease along the diagonals.

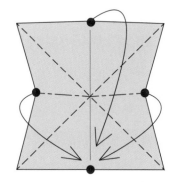

3 Collapse the paper to bring the three upper corners to the bottom corner.

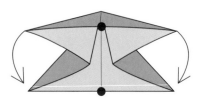

4 Step 3 in progress. Flatten the model.

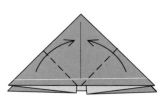

5 Valley fold the side flaps up to the top.

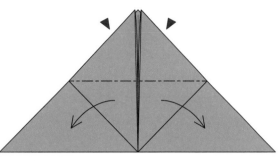

6 Open out the flaps and squash fold them flat.

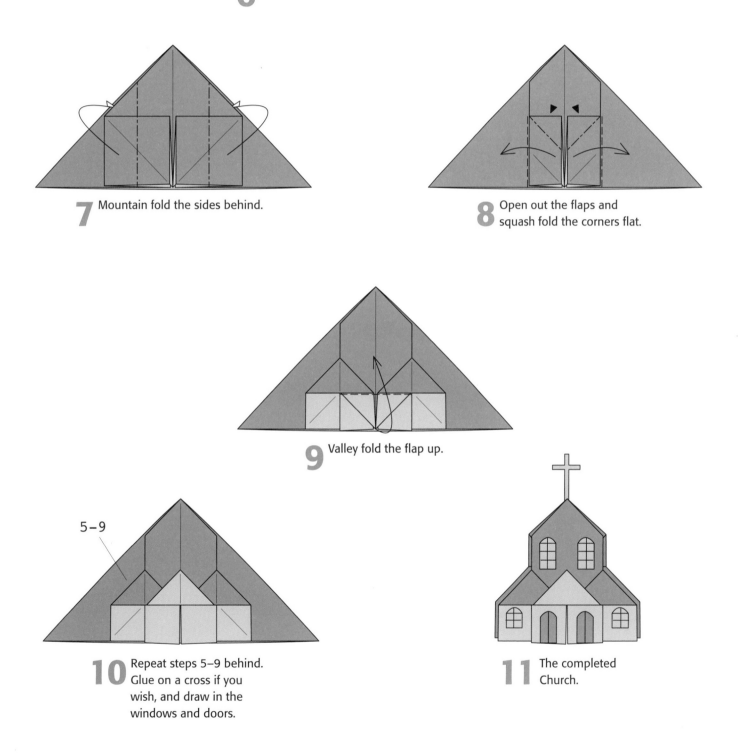

7 Mountain fold the sides behind.

8 Open out the flaps and squash fold the corners flat.

9 Valley fold the flap up.

5–9

10 Repeat steps 5–9 behind. Glue on a cross if you wish, and draw in the windows and doors.

11 The completed Church.

Star Flowers

This is one versatile paper flower! Simply changing the color scheme can suggest a wide variety of blossoms. Use a yellow and gold combination for a sunflower, or perhaps violet and yellow for an aster. For a camellia, yellow with white works well. You can approximate several species that have large centers.

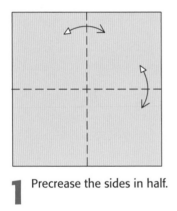

1 Precrease the sides in half.

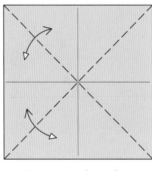

2 Precrease along the diagonals.

3 Valley fold the corners to the center, and then unfold them.

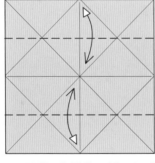

4 Valley fold the sides to the center, and unfold them.

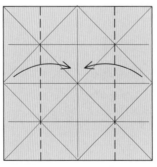

5 Valley fold the sides to the center.

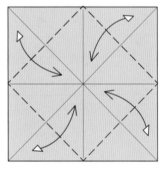

6 Inside-reverse fold the four corners.

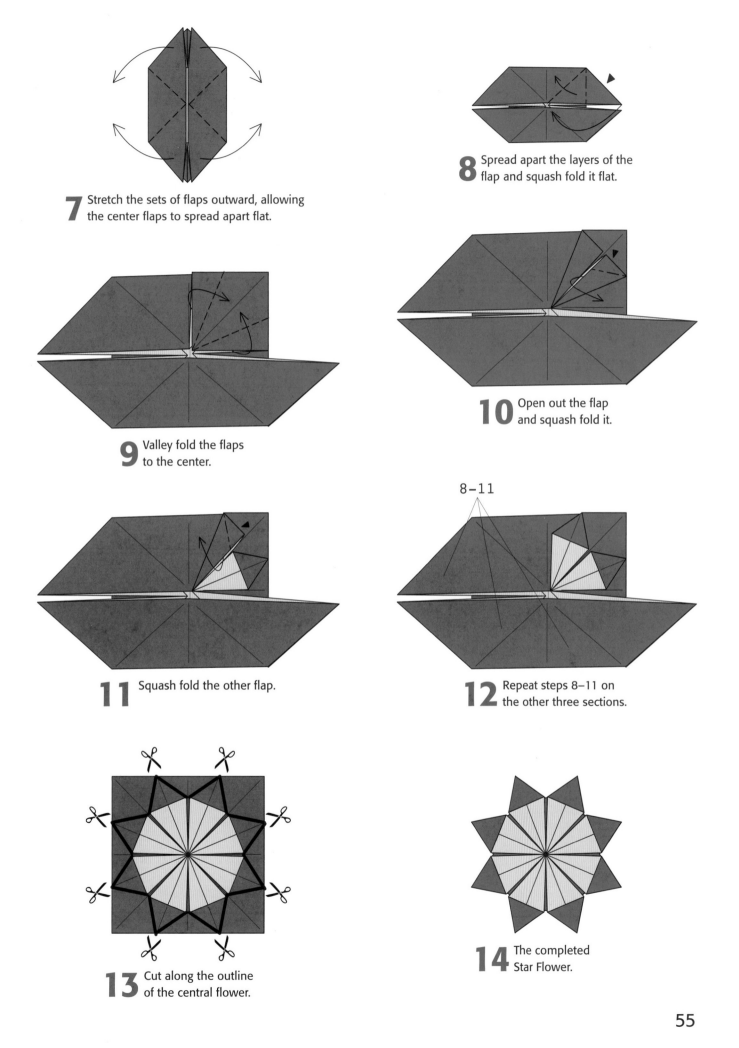

7 Stretch the sets of flaps outward, allowing the center flaps to spread apart flat.

8 Spread apart the layers of the flap and squash fold it flat.

9 Valley fold the flaps to the center.

10 Open out the flap and squash fold it.

11 Squash fold the other flap.

8–11

12 Repeat steps 8–11 on the other three sections.

13 Cut along the outline of the central flower.

14 The completed Star Flower.

Tents

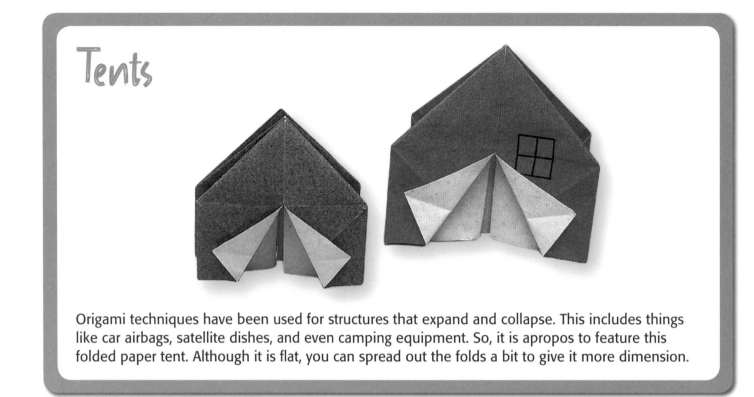

Origami techniques have been used for structures that expand and collapse. This includes things like car airbags, satellite dishes, and even camping equipment. So, it is apropos to feature this folded paper tent. Although it is flat, you can spread out the folds a bit to give it more dimension.

1 Precrease the sides in half. Turn the paper over.

2 Precrease along the diagonals.

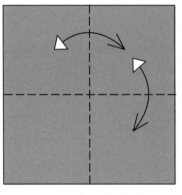

3 Collapse the paper to bring the three upper corners to the bottom corner.

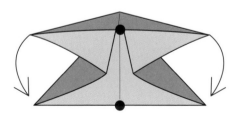

4 Step 3 in progress. Flatten the model.

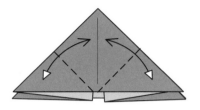

5 Precrease the flaps in half. Repeat behind.

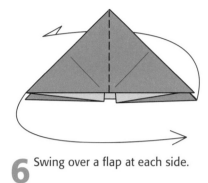

6 Swing over a flap at each side.

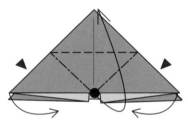

7 Pull the point identified with the dot to the top, allowing the sides to squash fold flat.

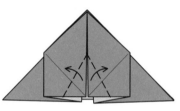

8 Valley fold the top layers outward.

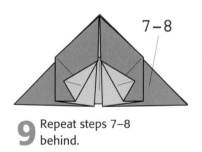

7–8

9 Repeat steps 7–8 behind.

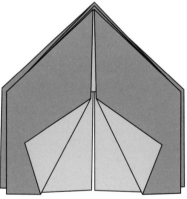

10 The completed Tent.

Candy Boxes

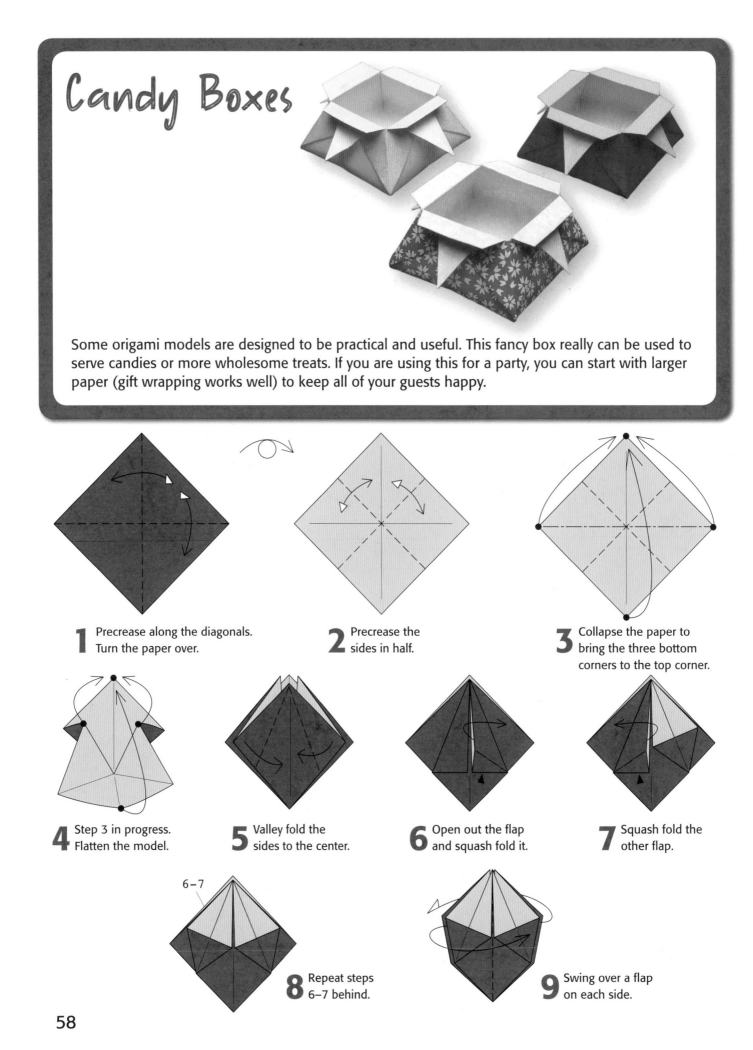

Some origami models are designed to be practical and useful. This fancy box really can be used to serve candies or more wholesome treats. If you are using this for a party, you can start with larger paper (gift wrapping works well) to keep all of your guests happy.

1 Precrease along the diagonals. Turn the paper over.

2 Precrease the sides in half.

3 Collapse the paper to bring the three bottom corners to the top corner.

4 Step 3 in progress. Flatten the model.

5 Valley fold the sides to the center.

6 Open out the flap and squash fold it.

7 Squash fold the other flap.

8 Repeat steps 6–7 behind.

9 Swing over a flap on each side.

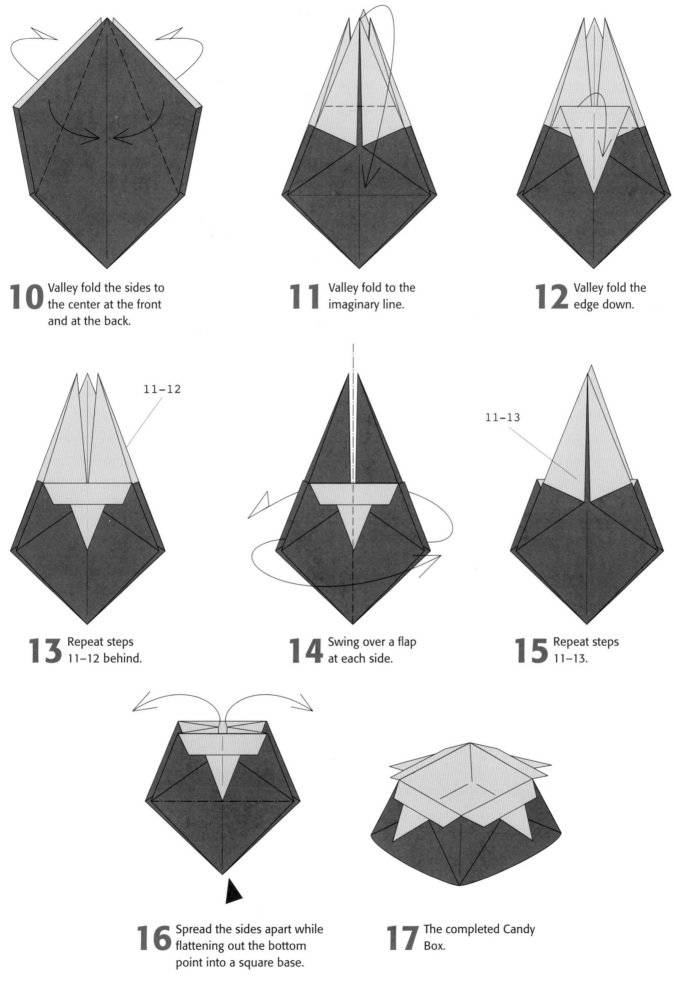

10 Valley fold the sides to the center at the front and at the back.

11 Valley fold to the imaginary line.

12 Valley fold the edge down.

11–12

13 Repeat steps 11–12 behind.

14 Swing over a flap at each side.

11–13

15 Repeat steps 11–13.

16 Spread the sides apart while flattening out the bottom point into a square base.

17 The completed Candy Box.

Piano

Back in the early 1800s, the advent of the upright piano brought the sound of its larger siblings into a far more compact form factor. These instruments became extremely popular and are still used today. You can recreate this keyboard through folding, and make it small enough to fit into a dollhouse.

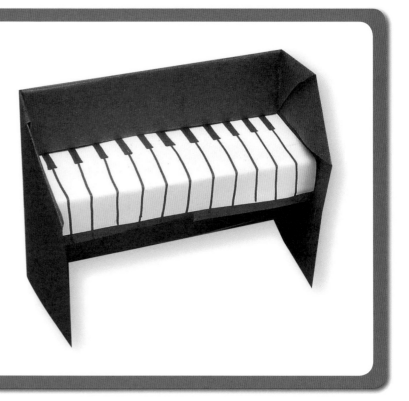

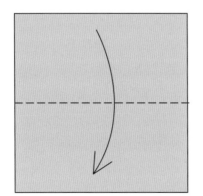

1 Valley fold in half.

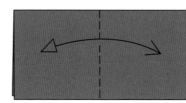

2 Precrease in half.

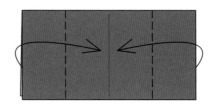

3 Valley fold the sides to the center.

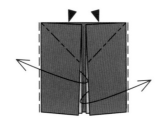

4 Open out the top layers and squash fold the corners.

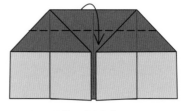

5 Valley fold the top section in half.

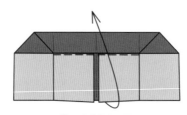

6 Valley fold the flap up.

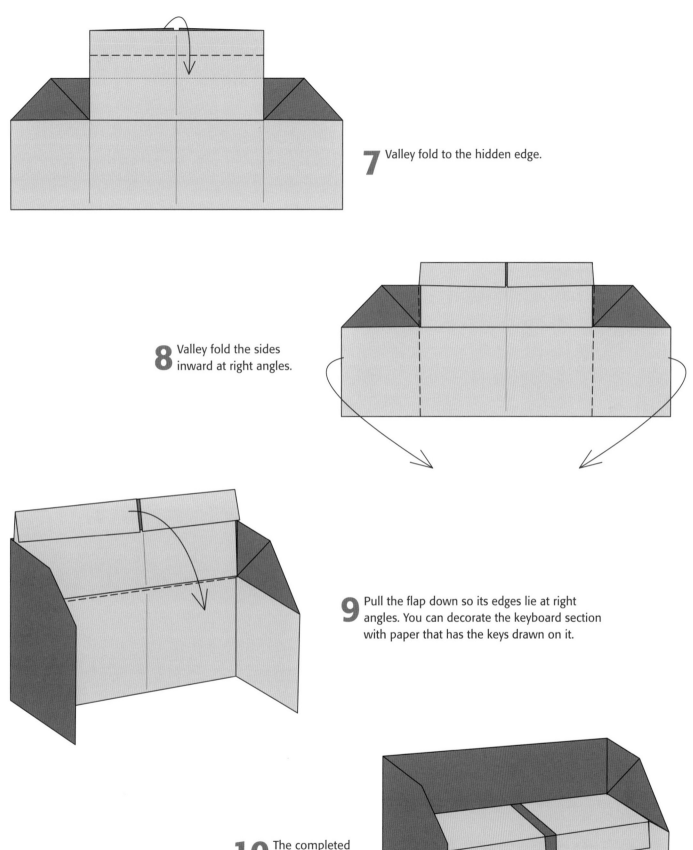

7 Valley fold to the hidden edge.

8 Valley fold the sides inward at right angles.

9 Pull the flap down so its edges lie at right angles. You can decorate the keyboard section with paper that has the keys drawn on it.

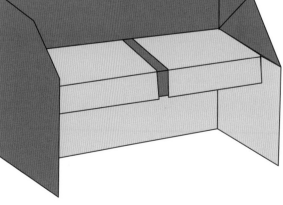

10 The completed Piano.

Caps

Both caps look charming when made with normal sized origami paper, but they are even more exciting if you use larger paper so you can wear them! To get a good fit, use a square sheet of paper that has a width equal to the circumference of your head. You can even use these as part of a Halloween costume.

Nurse's Cap

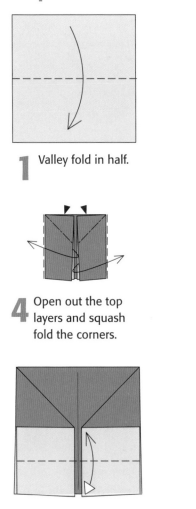

1 Valley fold in half.

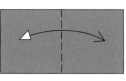

2 Precrease in half.

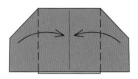

3 Valley fold the sides to the center.

4 Open out the top layers and squash fold the corners.

5 Turn the paper over.

6 Valley fold the sides to the center.

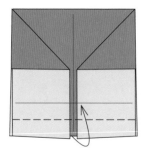

7 Precrease the top flap in half.

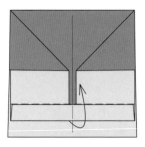

8 Valley fold to the crease from step 7.

9 Valley fold along the existing crease.

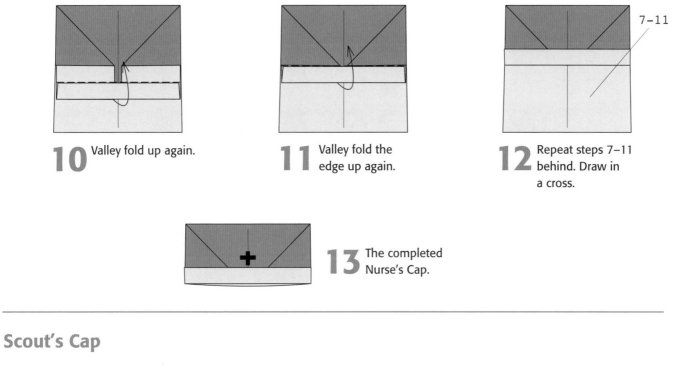

10 Valley fold up again.

11 Valley fold the edge up again.

12 Repeat steps 7–11 behind. Draw in a cross.

13 The completed Nurse's Cap.

Scout's Cap

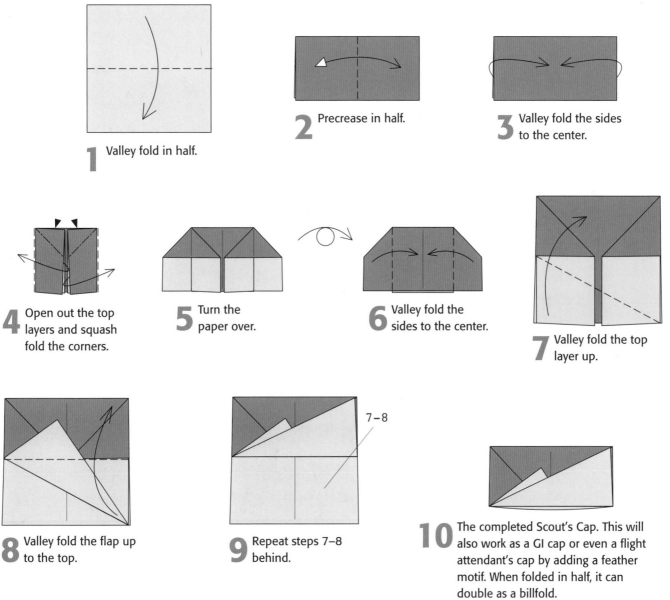

1 Valley fold in half.

2 Precrease in half.

3 Valley fold the sides to the center.

4 Open out the top layers and squash fold the corners.

5 Turn the paper over.

6 Valley fold the sides to the center.

7 Valley fold the top layer up.

8 Valley fold the flap up to the top.

9 Repeat steps 7–8 behind.

10 The completed Scout's Cap. This will also work as a GI cap or even a flight attendant's cap by adding a feather motif. When folded in half, it can double as a billfold.

Birds

This traditional origami bird was introduced as a dove when it was first published back in 1931. Because it sports a belly of a contrasting color, you can take advantage of this feature to have it represent other fowl like bluebirds, robins or chats. This would be a great use of duo papers, with unique colors on each side.

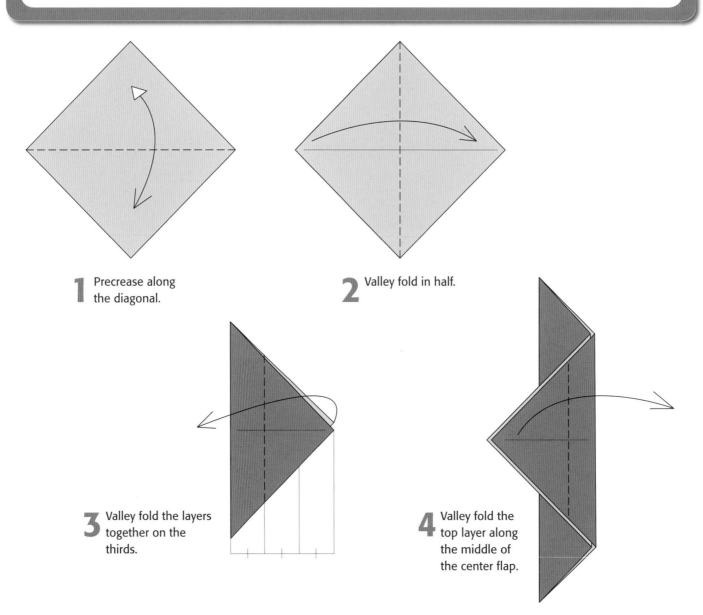

1 Precrease along the diagonal.

2 Valley fold in half.

3 Valley fold the layers together on the thirds.

4 Valley fold the top layer along the middle of the center flap.

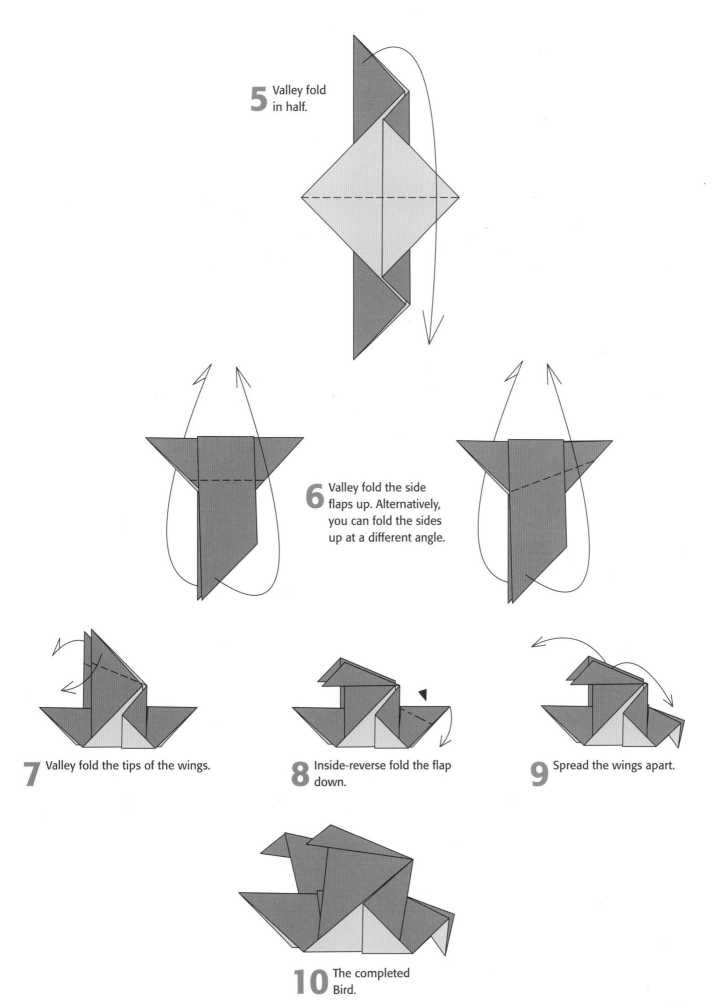

5 Valley fold in half.

6 Valley fold the side flaps up. Alternatively, you can fold the sides up at a different angle.

7 Valley fold the tips of the wings.

8 Inside-reverse fold the flap down.

9 Spread the wings apart.

10 The completed Bird.

Whale

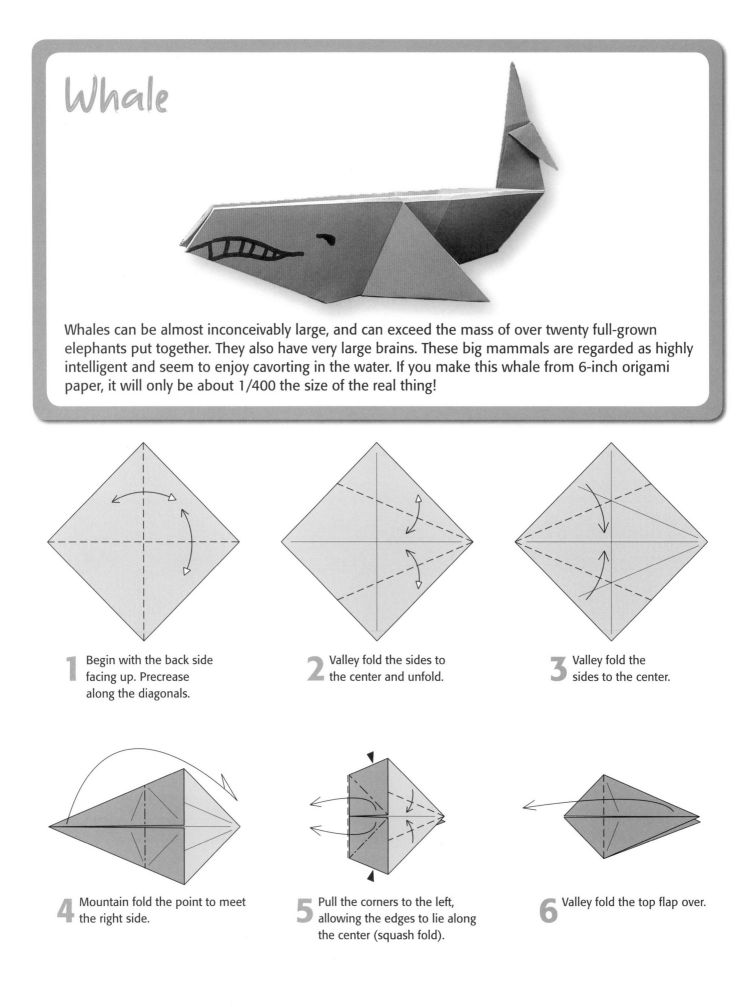

Whales can be almost inconceivably large, and can exceed the mass of over twenty full-grown elephants put together. They also have very large brains. These big mammals are regarded as highly intelligent and seem to enjoy cavorting in the water. If you make this whale from 6-inch origami paper, it will only be about 1/400 the size of the real thing!

1 Begin with the back side facing up. Precrease along the diagonals.

2 Valley fold the sides to the center and unfold.

3 Valley fold the sides to the center.

4 Mountain fold the point to meet the right side.

5 Pull the corners to the left, allowing the edges to lie along the center (squash fold).

6 Valley fold the top flap over.

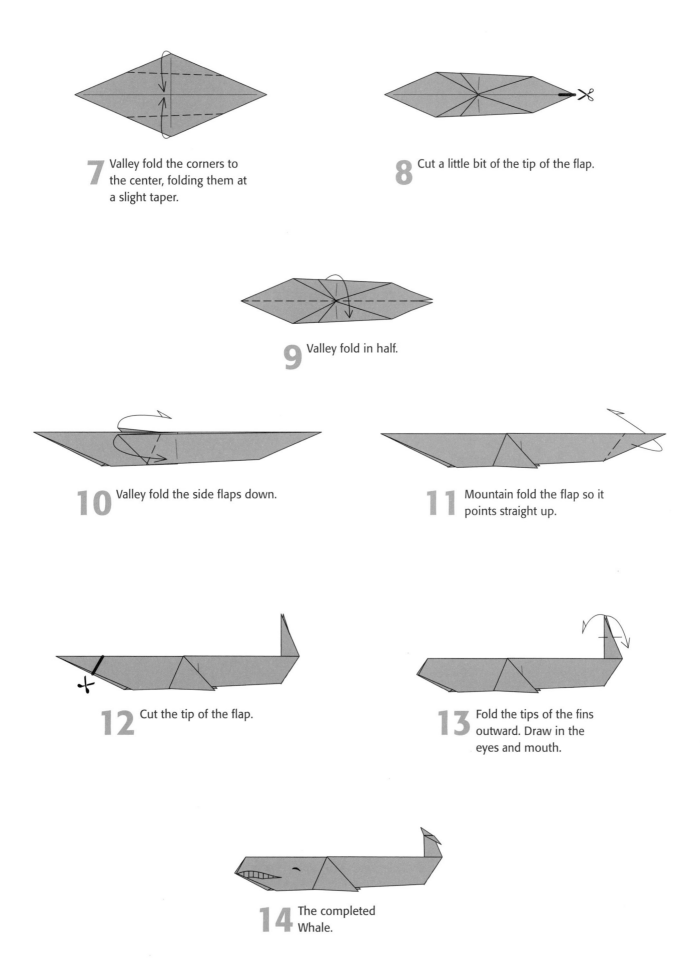

7 Valley fold the corners to the center, folding them at a slight taper.

8 Cut a little bit of the tip of the flap.

9 Valley fold in half.

10 Valley fold the side flaps down.

11 Mountain fold the flap so it points straight up.

12 Cut the tip of the flap.

13 Fold the tips of the fins outward. Draw in the eyes and mouth.

14 The completed Whale.

Swallow

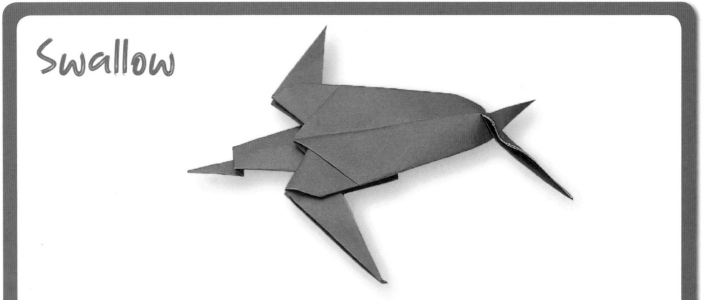

Swallows will arrive in Japan at the beginning of spring like clockwork. The bird is used as a motif for many seasonal decorations. They have come to represent loyalty and fertility as this species will mate for life. Fold one of these elegant birds for yourself or to give as a gift.

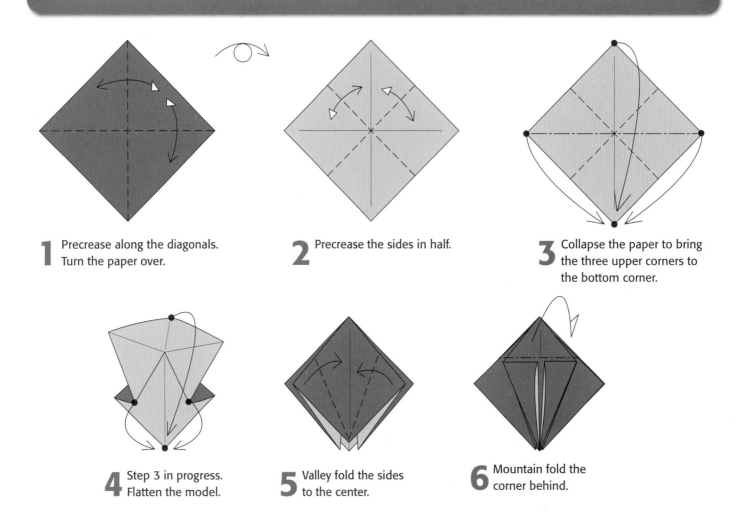

1 Precrease along the diagonals. Turn the paper over.

2 Precrease the sides in half.

3 Collapse the paper to bring the three upper corners to the bottom corner.

4 Step 3 in progress. Flatten the model.

5 Valley fold the sides to the center.

6 Mountain fold the corner behind.

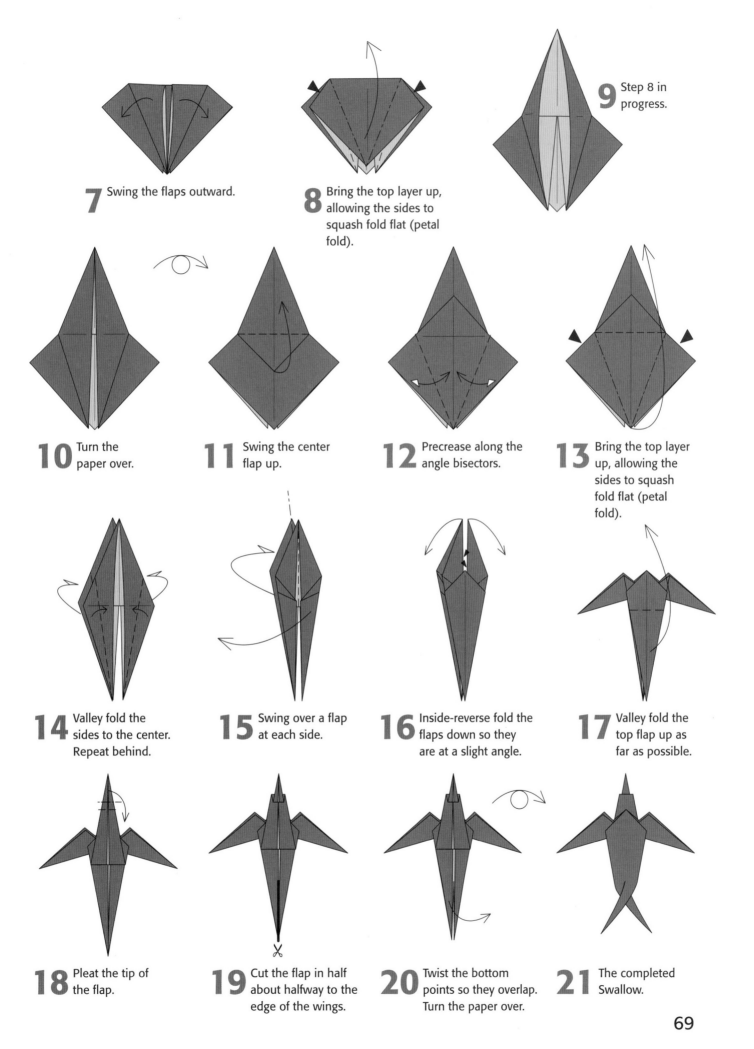

7 Swing the flaps outward.

8 Bring the top layer up, allowing the sides to squash fold flat (petal fold).

9 Step 8 in progress.

10 Turn the paper over.

11 Swing the center flap up.

12 Precrease along the angle bisectors.

13 Bring the top layer up, allowing the sides to squash fold flat (petal fold).

14 Valley fold the sides to the center. Repeat behind.

15 Swing over a flap at each side.

16 Inside-reverse fold the flaps down so they are at a slight angle.

17 Valley fold the top flap up as far as possible.

18 Pleat the tip of the flap.

19 Cut the flap in half about halfway to the edge of the wings.

20 Twist the bottom points so they overlap. Turn the paper over.

21 The completed Swallow.

Frogs

In Japanese, the words for "frog" and "return" happen to sound alike. Because of this, models of frogs are commonly placed in store windows to bring good fortune. Making this origami version might bring you some good fortune, too!

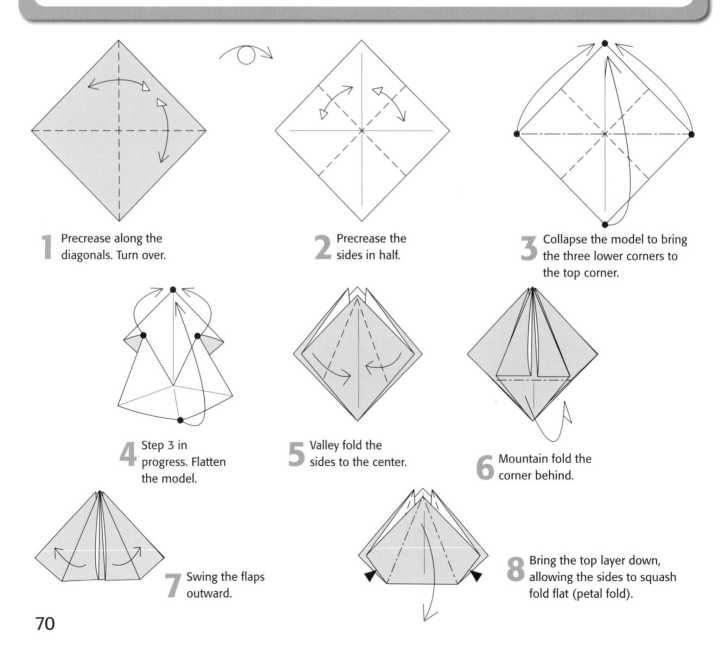

1 Precrease along the diagonals. Turn over.

2 Precrease the sides in half.

3 Collapse the model to bring the three lower corners to the top corner.

4 Step 3 in progress. Flatten the model.

5 Valley fold the sides to the center.

6 Mountain fold the corner behind.

7 Swing the flaps outward.

8 Bring the top layer down, allowing the sides to squash fold flat (petal fold).

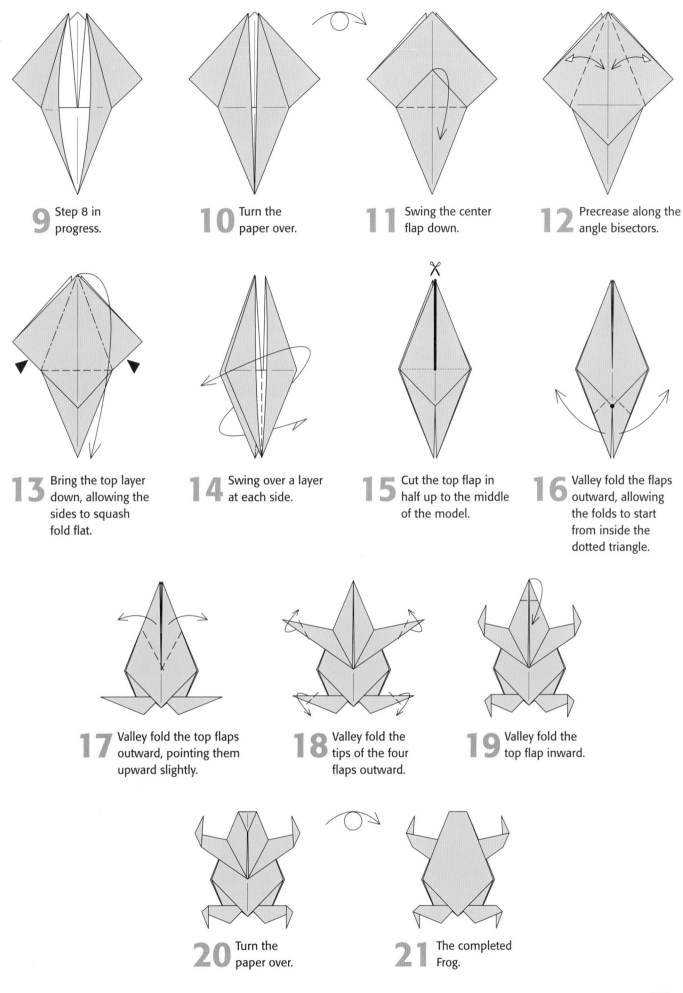

9 Step 8 in progress.

10 Turn the paper over.

11 Swing the center flap down.

12 Precrease along the angle bisectors.

13 Bring the top layer down, allowing the sides to squash fold flat.

14 Swing over a layer at each side.

15 Cut the top flap in half up to the middle of the model.

16 Valley fold the flaps outward, allowing the folds to start from inside the dotted triangle.

17 Valley fold the top flaps outward, pointing them upward slightly.

18 Valley fold the tips of the four flaps outward.

19 Valley fold the top flap inward.

20 Turn the paper over.

21 The completed Frog.

Prince and Princess

The Heian period in Japan is considered a cultural high point, beginning in 794 CE. The formal dress of this time was lavish, with many layers of fabric sporting intricate patterns. The nobility took this to extremes. These origami depictions of a Prince and Princess celebrate this opulent time.

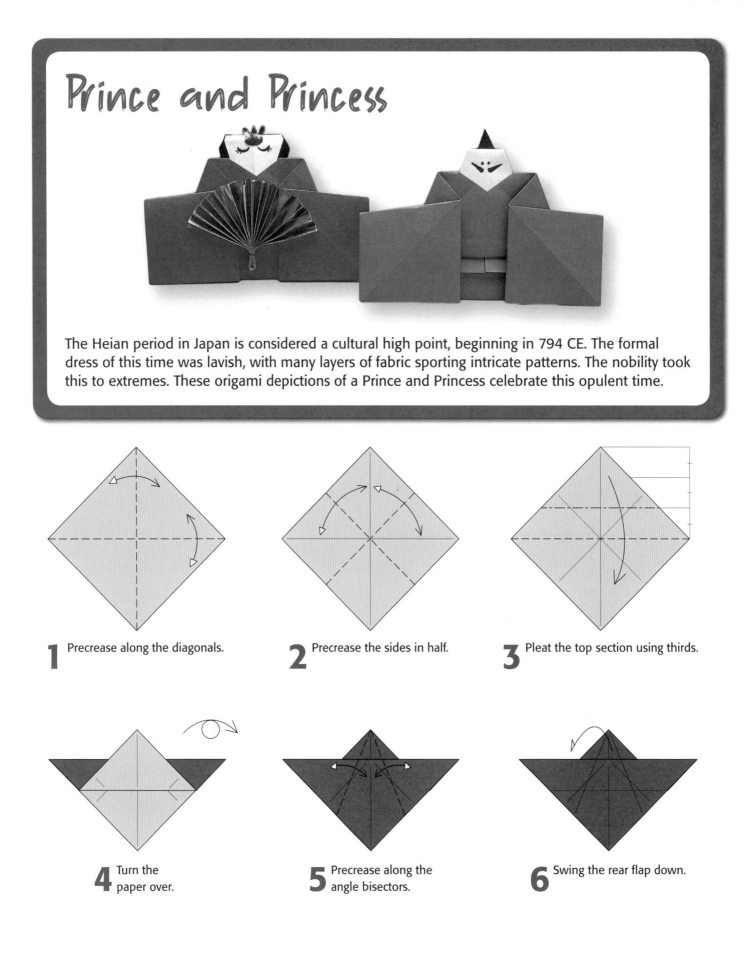

1 Precrease along the diagonals.

2 Precrease the sides in half.

3 Pleat the top section using thirds.

4 Turn the paper over.

5 Precrease along the angle bisectors.

6 Swing the rear flap down.

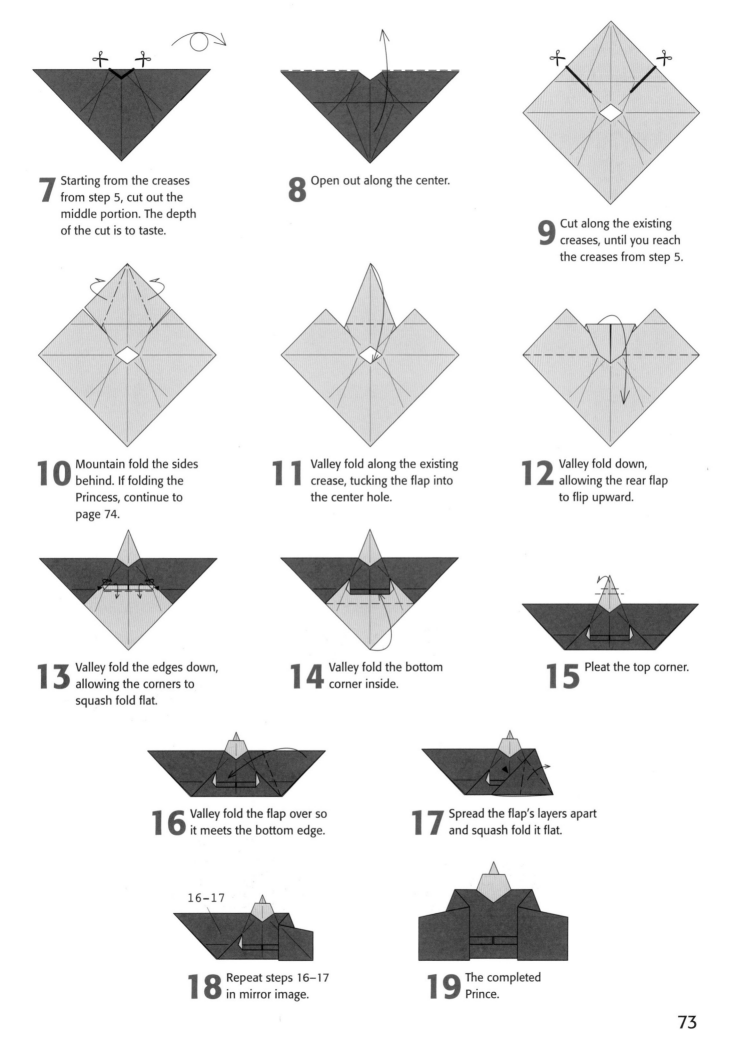

7 Starting from the creases from step 5, cut out the middle portion. The depth of the cut is to taste.

8 Open out along the center.

9 Cut along the existing creases, until you reach the creases from step 5.

10 Mountain fold the sides behind. If folding the Princess, continue to page 74.

11 Valley fold along the existing crease, tucking the flap into the center hole.

12 Valley fold down, allowing the rear flap to flip upward.

13 Valley fold the edges down, allowing the corners to squash fold flat.

14 Valley fold the bottom corner inside.

15 Pleat the top corner.

16 Valley fold the flap over so it meets the bottom edge.

17 Spread the flap's layers apart and squash fold it flat.

16–17

18 Repeat steps 16–17 in mirror image.

19 The completed Prince.

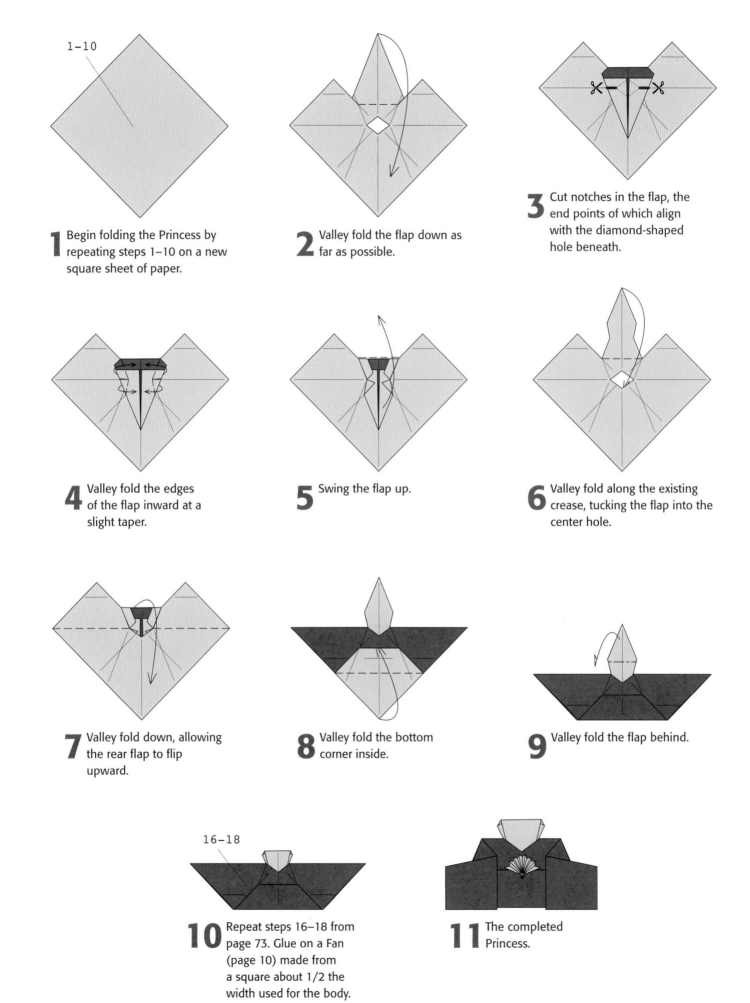

1 Begin folding the Princess by repeating steps 1–10 on a new square sheet of paper.

2 Valley fold the flap down as far as possible.

3 Cut notches in the flap, the end points of which align with the diamond-shaped hole beneath.

4 Valley fold the edges of the flap inward at a slight taper.

5 Swing the flap up.

6 Valley fold along the existing crease, tucking the flap into the center hole.

7 Valley fold down, allowing the rear flap to flip upward.

8 Valley fold the bottom corner inside.

9 Valley fold the flap behind.

10 Repeat steps 16–18 from page 73. Glue on a Fan (page 10) made from a square about 1/2 the width used for the body.

11 The completed Princess.

Pig

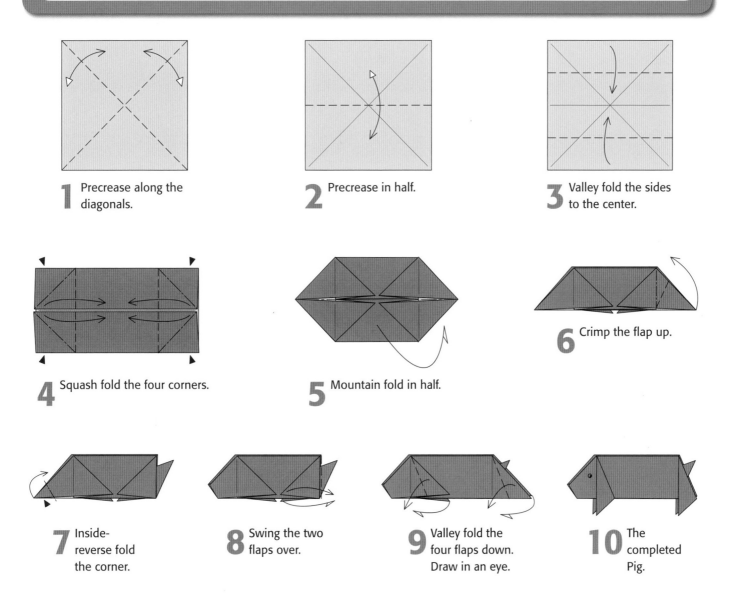

Wild pigs roam the mountains of Japan, and they've developed a reputation for being dangerous and unpredictable. In folklore, the boar came to be known as a symbol of prosperity. Domesticated pigs are arguably cuter, which is what this origami model is based on.

1 Precrease along the diagonals.

2 Precrease in half.

3 Valley fold the sides to the center.

4 Squash fold the four corners.

5 Mountain fold in half.

6 Crimp the flap up.

7 Inside-reverse fold the corner.

8 Swing the two flaps over.

9 Valley fold the four flaps down. Draw in an eye.

10 The completed Pig.

Motorboats

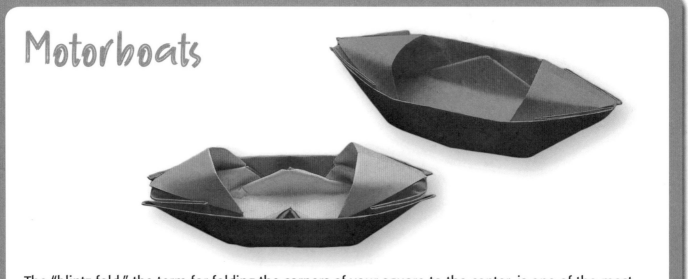

The "blintz fold," the term for folding the corners of your square to the center, is one of the most important origami design techniques. The corners can be pulled out and manipulated later in the folding sequence. It is the power of this technique that transforms the simpler Canoe (page 90) into this more impressive model.

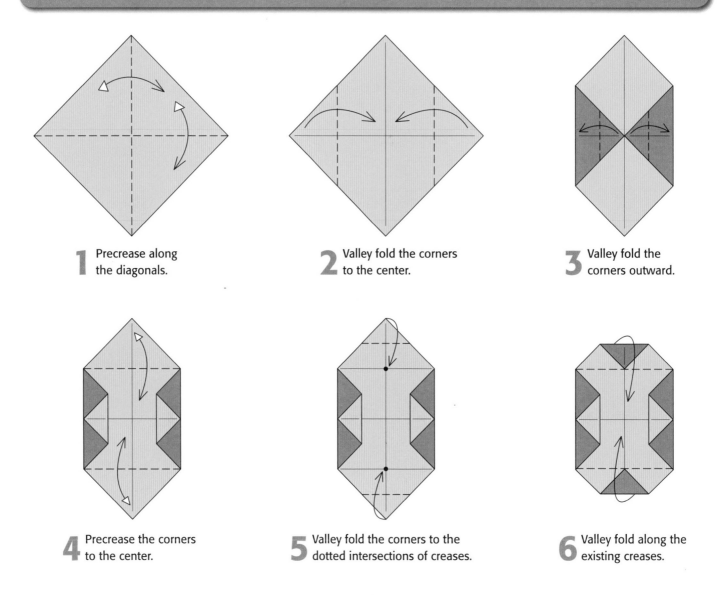

1 Precrease along the diagonals.

2 Valley fold the corners to the center.

3 Valley fold the corners outward.

4 Precrease the corners to the center.

5 Valley fold the corners to the dotted intersections of creases.

6 Valley fold along the existing creases.

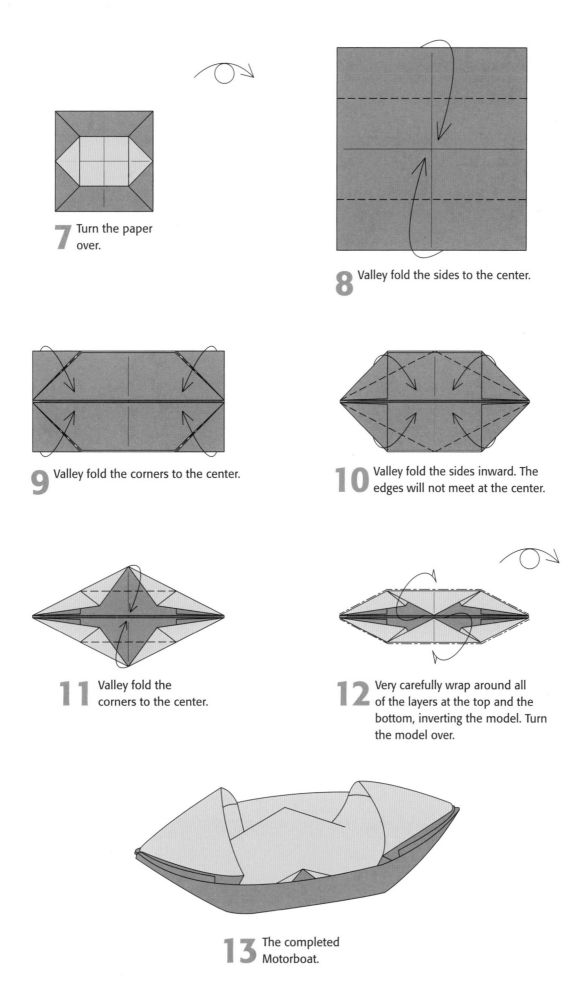

7 Turn the paper over.

8 Valley fold the sides to the center.

9 Valley fold the corners to the center.

10 Valley fold the sides inward. The edges will not meet at the center.

11 Valley fold the corners to the center.

12 Very carefully wrap around all of the layers at the top and the bottom, inverting the model. Turn the model over.

13 The completed Motorboat.

Jet Plane

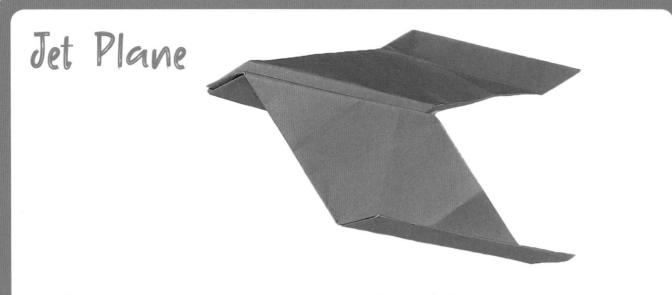

Not all paper planes are designed to fly. Some, like this jet, are designed to just *look* like they are flying. With its arched back wings, it exudes speed more than most schoolyard paper darts. Hanging it from a mobile gives a great effect.

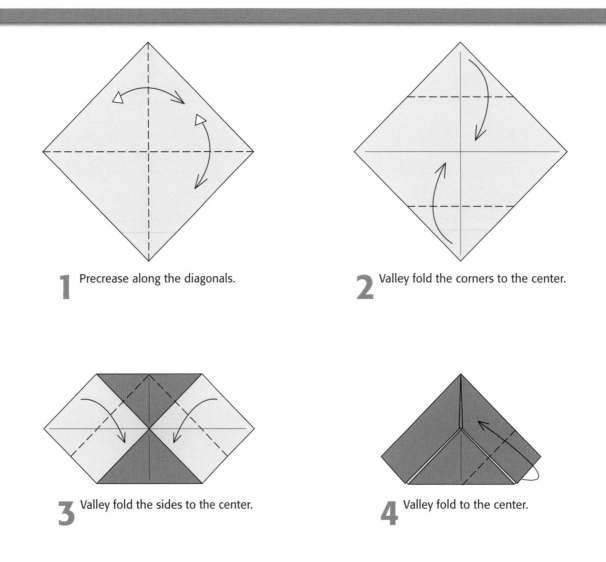

1 Precrease along the diagonals.

2 Valley fold the corners to the center.

3 Valley fold the sides to the center.

4 Valley fold to the center.

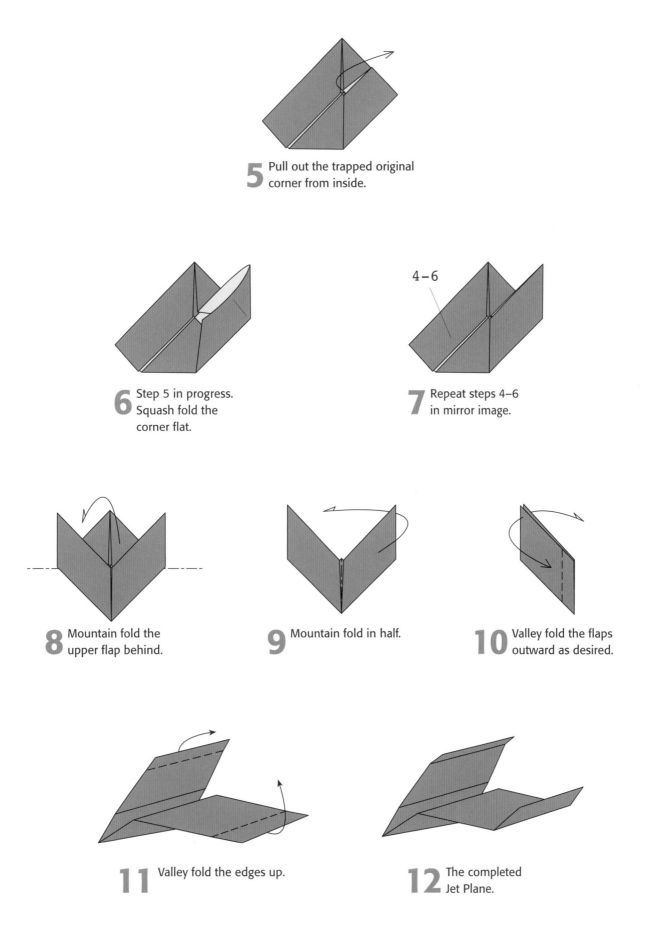

5 Pull out the trapped original corner from inside.

6 Step 5 in progress. Squash fold the corner flat.

4–6

7 Repeat steps 4–6 in mirror image.

8 Mountain fold the upper flap behind.

9 Mountain fold in half.

10 Valley fold the flaps outward as desired.

11 Valley fold the edges up.

12 The completed Jet Plane.

Table

Much of origami design is about having the structure and form of your subject conform to the geometry of your square paper. Occasionally a subject presents itself that requires very little work to accomplish this transformation. This table is one of those rare examples, where the four corners become legs and are simply folded at right angles. The interesting sequence makes this otherwise straightforward metamorphosis fun to fold.

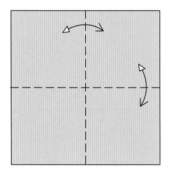

1 Precrease the sides in half.

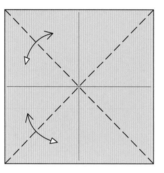

2 Precrease along the diagonals.

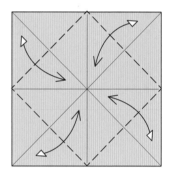

3 Valley fold the corners to the center, and then unfold them.

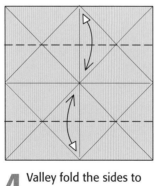

4 Valley fold the sides to the center, and then unfold them.

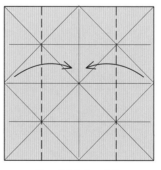

5 Valley fold the sides to the center.

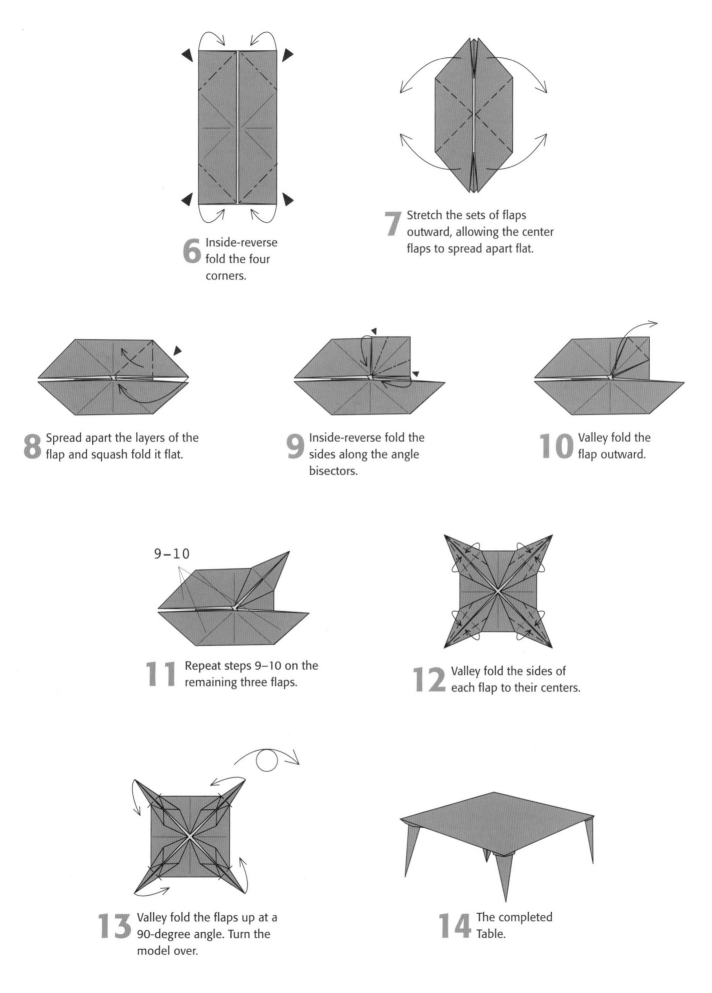

6 Inside-reverse fold the four corners.

7 Stretch the sets of flaps outward, allowing the center flaps to spread apart flat.

8 Spread apart the layers of the flap and squash fold it flat.

9 Inside-reverse fold the sides along the angle bisectors.

10 Valley fold the flap outward.

9–10

11 Repeat steps 9–10 on the remaining three flaps.

12 Valley fold the sides of each flap to their centers.

13 Valley fold the flaps up at a 90-degree angle. Turn the model over.

14 The completed Table.

Spaceship

Space travel has captured the imaginations of everyone, both young and old. Since the effects of gravity are minimal after leaving earth, spacecraft can take on a wide variety of creative forms. This origami one sports a double set of wings so it can navigate comfortably upon entering a planet's atmosphere.

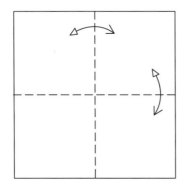

1 Precrease the sides in half.

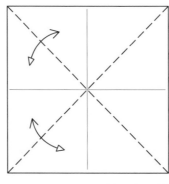

2 Precrease the sides in half.

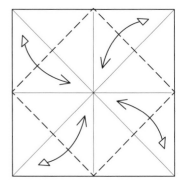

3 Valley fold the corners to the center and then unfold them.

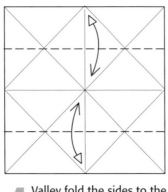

4 Valley fold the sides to the center, and then unfold them.

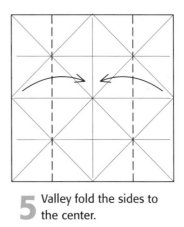

5 Valley fold the sides to the center.

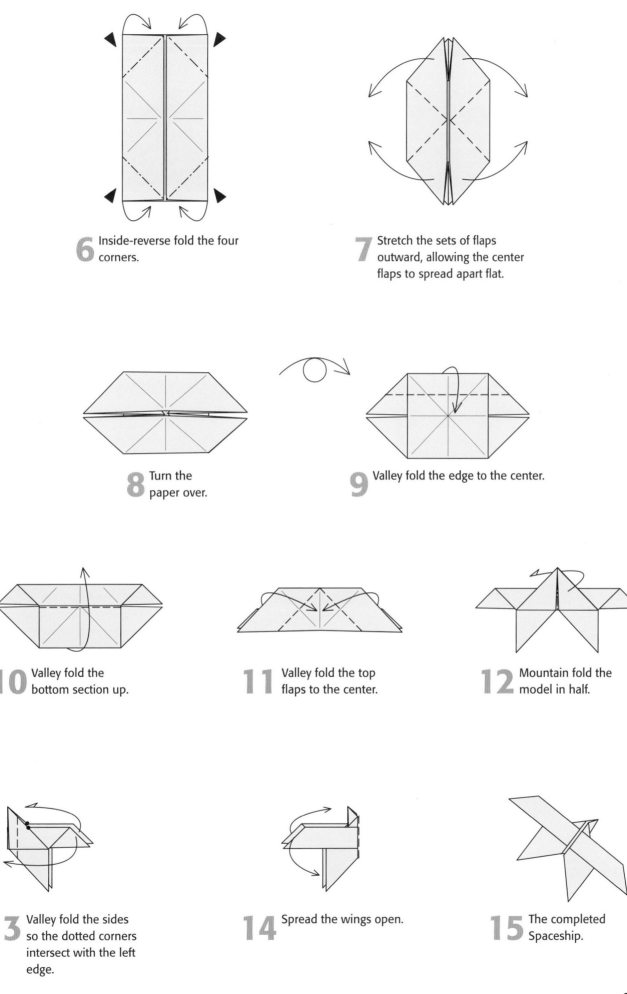

6 Inside-reverse fold the four corners.

7 Stretch the sets of flaps outward, allowing the center flaps to spread apart flat.

8 Turn the paper over.

9 Valley fold the edge to the center.

10 Valley fold the bottom section up.

11 Valley fold the top flaps to the center.

12 Mountain fold the model in half.

13 Valley fold the sides so the dotted corners intersect with the left edge.

14 Spread the wings open.

15 The completed Spaceship.

Penguin

Penguins rightfully enjoy popularity as being one of the cutest animals ever to waddle the earth. They give off an air of carefree clumsiness all while looking formal with their tuxedo patterned body. This paper penguin exhibits a classic pose with its head turned up.

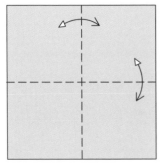

1 Precrease the sides in half.

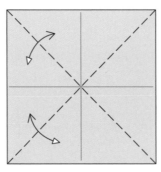

2 Precrease along the diagonals.

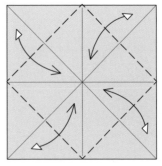

3 Valley fold the corners to the center, and then unfold them.

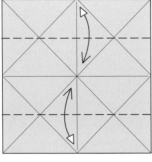

4 Valley fold the sides to the center, and then unfold them.

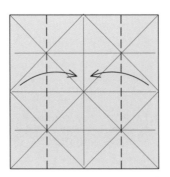

5 Valley fold the sides to the center.

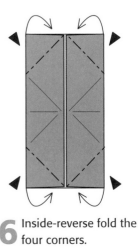

6 Inside-reverse fold the four corners.

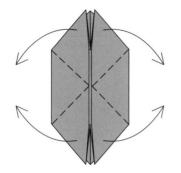

7 Stretch the sets of flaps outward, allowing the center flaps to spread apart flat.

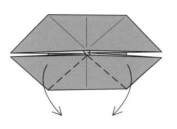

8 Swing the side flaps down.

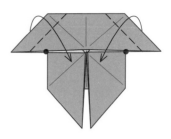

9 Valley fold the flaps so their edges intersect the dotted corners.

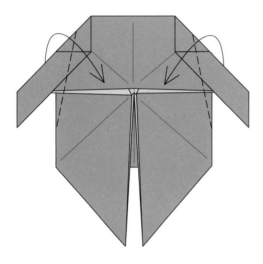

10 Valley fold the flaps inward so they lie somewhere along the middles of the sides.

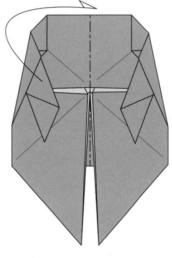

11 Mountain fold in half.

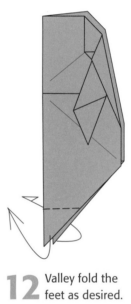

12 Valley fold the feet as desired.

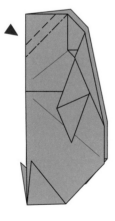

13 Inside-reverse fold the corner in and then out.

14 Detail of the head. Draw in dots at each side for eyes. Open out the feet.

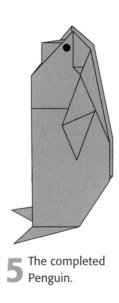

15 The completed Penguin.

85

Chairs

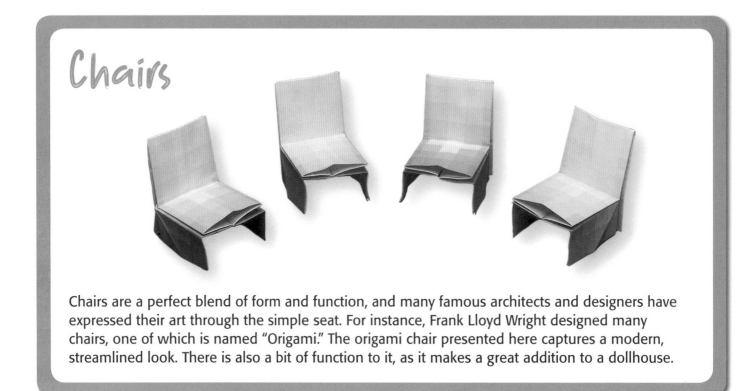

Chairs are a perfect blend of form and function, and many famous architects and designers have expressed their art through the simple seat. For instance, Frank Lloyd Wright designed many chairs, one of which is named "Origami." The origami chair presented here captures a modern, streamlined look. There is also a bit of function to it, as it makes a great addition to a dollhouse.

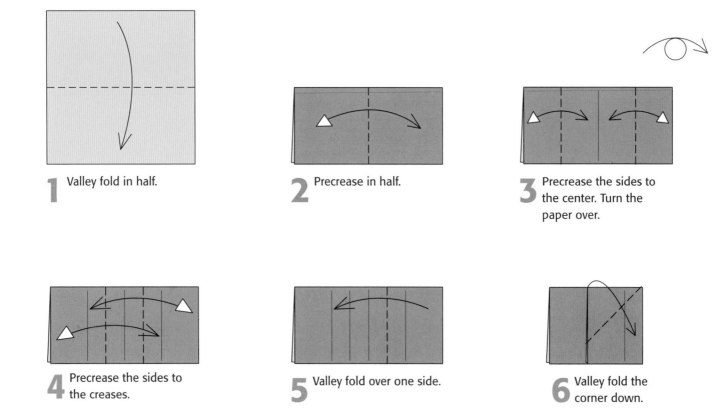

1 Valley fold in half.

2 Precrease in half.

3 Precrease the sides to the center. Turn the paper over.

4 Precrease the sides to the creases.

5 Valley fold over one side.

6 Valley fold the corner down.

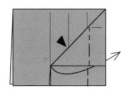

7 Inside-reverse fold the side through.

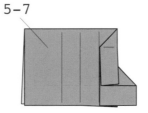

8 Repeat steps 5–7 in mirror image.

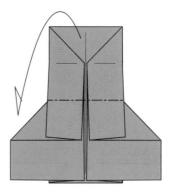

9 Mountain fold the top section behind.

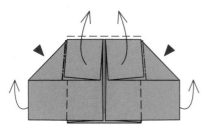

10 Raise the sides up into a box shape, pushing in at the arrows.

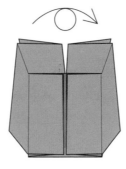

11 Turn the paper over.

12 Raise the top flap up.

13 The completed Chair.

Treasure Boxes

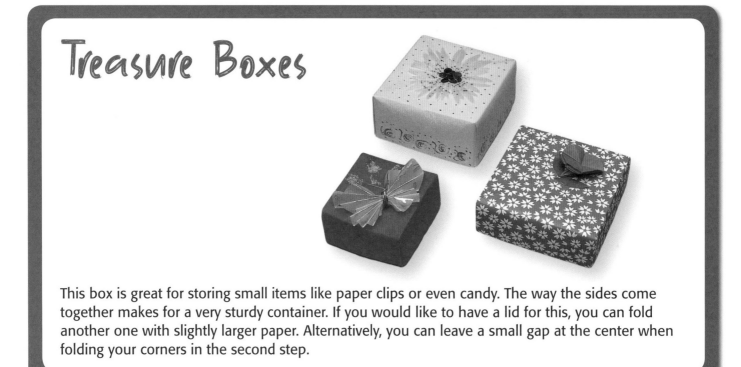

This box is great for storing small items like paper clips or even candy. The way the sides come together makes for a very sturdy container. If you would like to have a lid for this, you can fold another one with slightly larger paper. Alternatively, you can leave a small gap at the center when folding your corners in the second step.

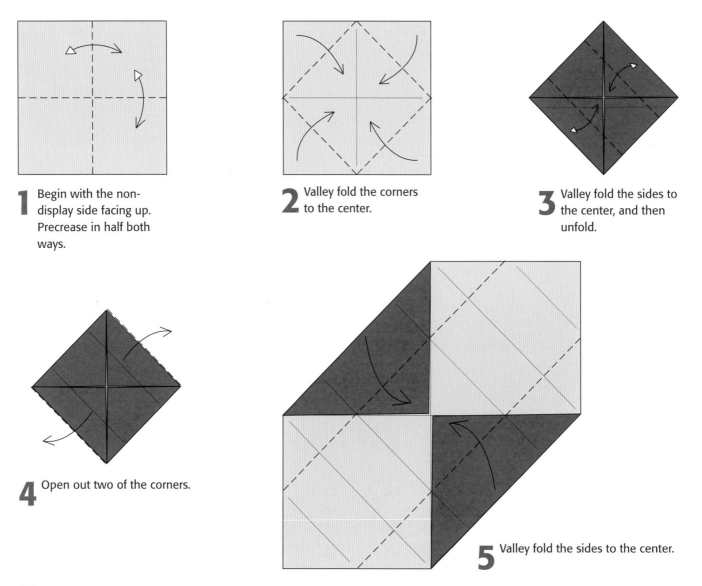

1 Begin with the non-display side facing up. Precrease in half both ways.

2 Valley fold the corners to the center.

3 Valley fold the sides to the center, and then unfold.

4 Open out two of the corners.

5 Valley fold the sides to the center.

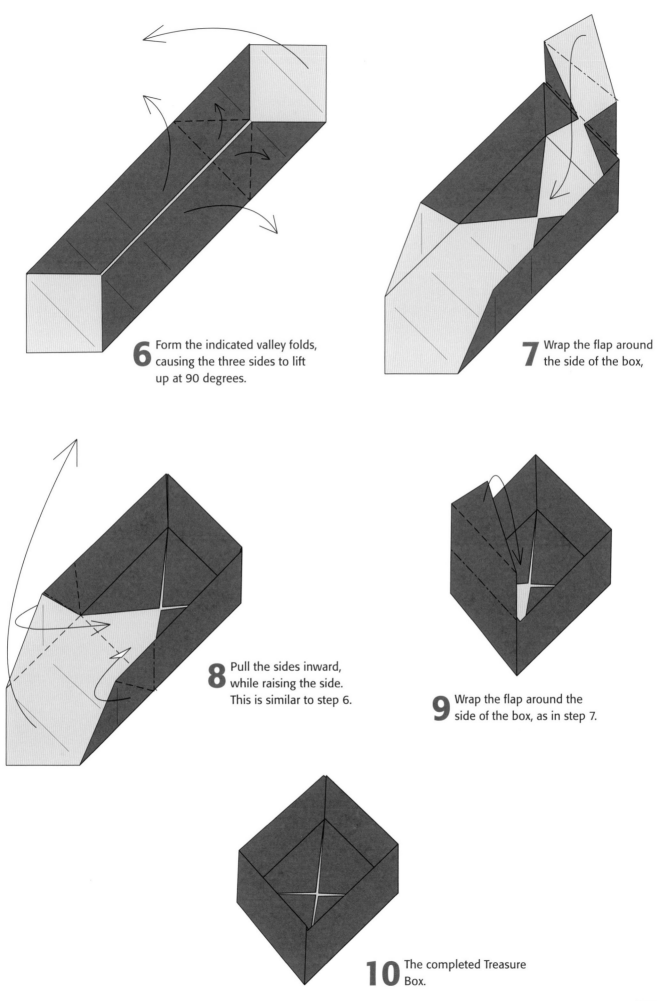

6 Form the indicated valley folds, causing the three sides to lift up at 90 degrees.

7 Wrap the flap around the side of the box,

8 Pull the sides inward, while raising the side. This is similar to step 6.

9 Wrap the flap around the side of the box, as in step 7.

10 The completed Treasure Box.

Canoes

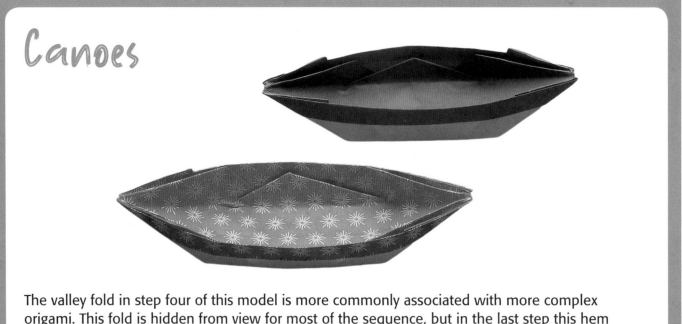

The valley fold in step four of this model is more commonly associated with more complex origami. This fold is hidden from view for most of the sequence, but in the last step this hem makes its appearance as a fancy stripe on the outside. If you use heavy paper this boat will float!

1 Precrease in half.

2 Make a pinch mark midway along the edge of the top and bottom sections.

3 Make a pinch mark midway along the edge of the uppermost and bottommost sections.

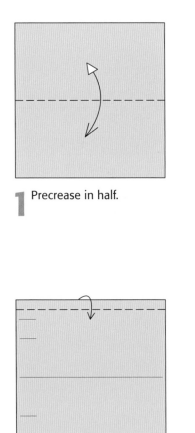

4 Valley fold the edges in, using the pinch marks from step 3 as the landmarks.

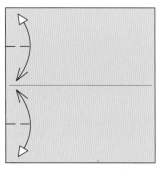

5 Valley fold the sides to the center.

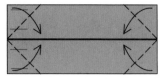

6 Valley fold the four corners to the center.

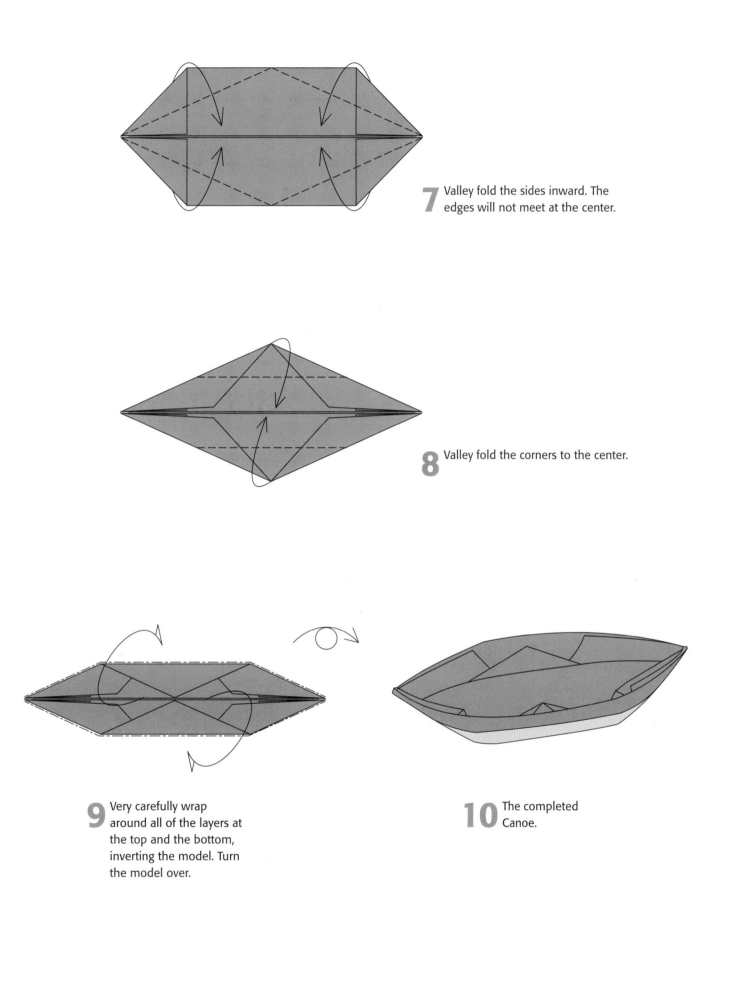

7 Valley fold the sides inward. The edges will not meet at the center.

8 Valley fold the corners to the center.

9 Very carefully wrap around all of the layers at the top and the bottom, inverting the model. Turn the model over.

10 The completed Canoe.

Using Origami Objects

Throwing a Party

On pages 92–95 you will find different ways of using the origami objects that you have learned to fold. Here are some party suggestions. These models are all from the book. Try to think of other ways to use these paper creations.

1 Lantern
p. 22

2 Star Flower
p. 54

3 Windmill
p. 24

4 Clown
p. 46

5 Flowers
p. 16

6 Treasure Box
p. 88

7 Swan
p. 26

8 Crane
p. 28

9 Wolf
p. 34

10 Cap
p. 62

11 Cat
p. 44

12 Samurai Helmet
p. 18

13 Dog
p. 32

14 Rabbit
p. 37

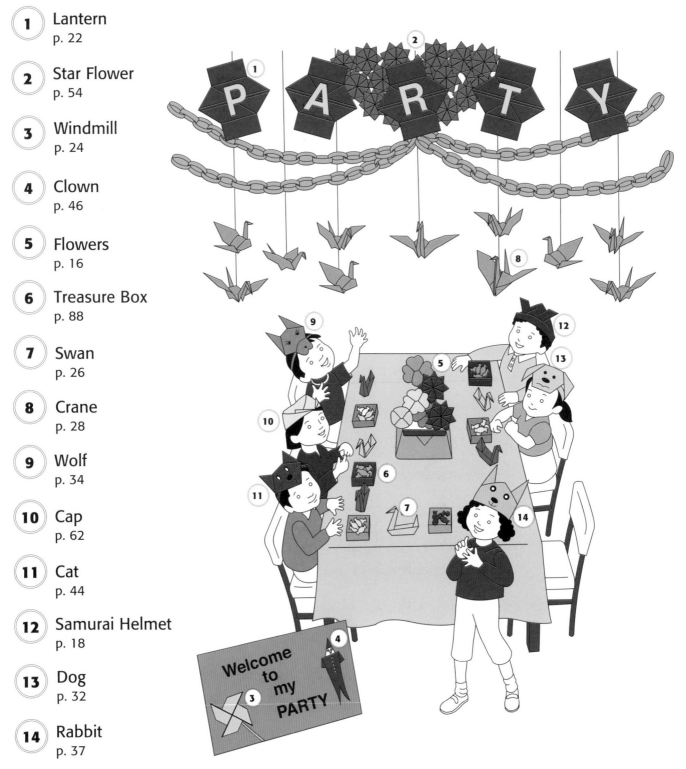

Making a Mobile

Make an origami mobile by stringing various objects of different sizes and colors to thin pieces of wire. The mobile shown here features birds, but any of the objects you have learned to fold can be used. (Never use an origami mobile over a crib—these models can be choking hazards!)

1 Swan
p. 26

2 Penguin
p. 84

3 Robin
p. 50

4 Peahen
p. 36

5 Peacock
p. 33

6 Swallow
p. 68

7 Crane
p. 28

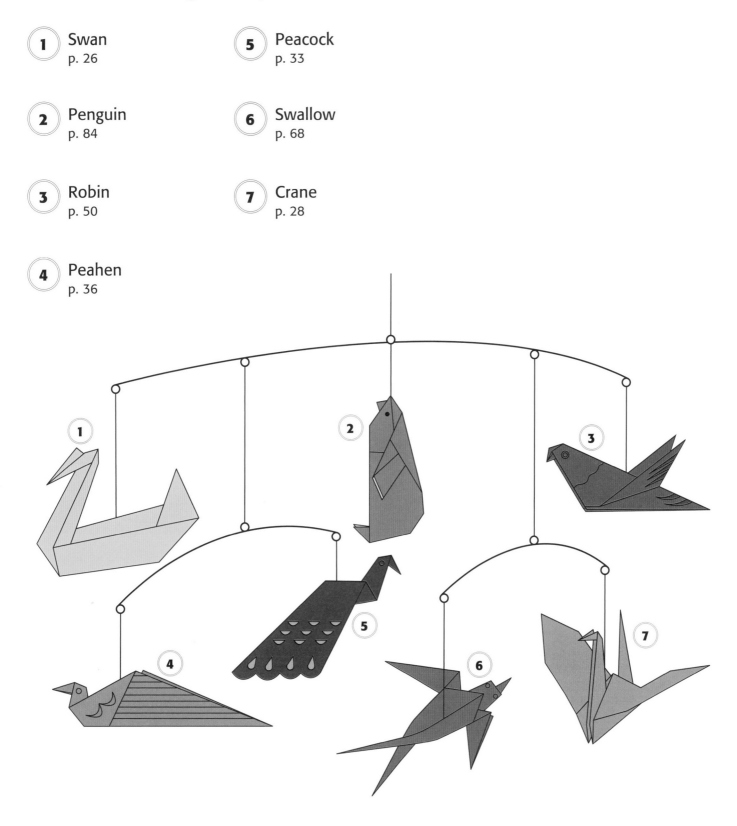

Organizing a Boat Race

Make boats of various sizes and colors. Tie or tape one end of a piece of string to each boat and the other end to the middle of a pencil. At the starting signal, each player winds the string on their pencil, thus reeling the boat in. The first boat reaching the finish line wins the race.

1 Motorboat
p. 76

2 Canoe
p. 90

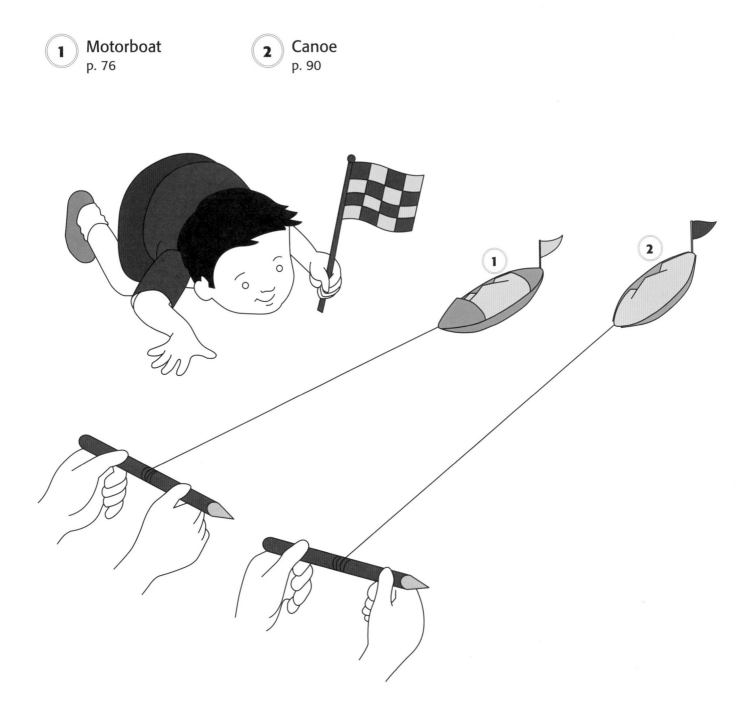

A Hunting Game

Arrange various origami objects on a table. Affix point values on each object, as shown in the example below. Stand at a distance from the table and, with a rubber band as a slingshot, shoot
these objects and let them fall. The one who gets the most points is the best hunter. Besides this hunting game, you can also make a miniature zoo with the different animals shown in the book.

1. Penguin
   p. 84

2. Whale
   p. 66

3. Giraffe
   p. 38

4. Peahen
   p. 36

5. Pig
   p. 75

6. Christmas Tree
   p. 14

7. Elephant
   p. 40

8. Rabbit
   p. 37

9. Tent
   p. 56

10. Wolf
    p. 34

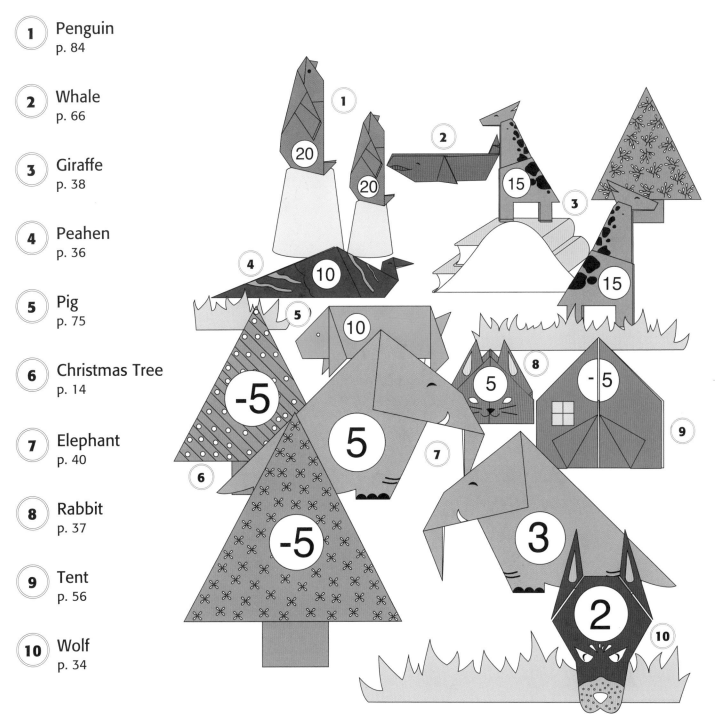

"Books to Span the East and West"

Tuttle Publishing was founded in 1832 in the small New England town of Rutland, Vermont [USA]. Our core values remain as strong today as they were then—to publish best-in-class books which bring people together one page at a time. In 1948, we established a publishing office in Japan—and Tuttle is now a leader in publishing English-language books about the arts, languages and cultures of Asia. The world has become a much smaller place today and Asia's economic and cultural influence has grown. Yet the need for meaningful dialogue and information about this diverse region has never been greater. Over the past seven decades, Tuttle has published thousands of books on subjects ranging from martial arts and paper crafts to language learning and literature—and our talented authors, illustrators, designers and photographers have won many prestigious awards. We welcome you to explore the wealth of information available on Asia at **www.tuttlepublishing.com**.

Published by Tuttle Publishing, an imprint of
Periplus Editions (HK) Ltd.

www.tuttlepublishing.com

Copyright © 1958, 1996, 2021 Charles E. Tuttle Company Inc.

All rights reserved.
Library of Congress Control Number: 2021937116

ISBN 978-0-8048-5445-0
ISBN 978-4-8053-1690-0 (for sale in Japan only)

First published in three volumes 1957–9
Second edition 2002

26 25 24 23 22
7 6 5 4 3 2   2212EP

Printed in China

Distributed by:

North America, Latin America & Europe
Tuttle Publishing
364 Innovation Drive
North Clarendon, VT 05759-9436 USA
Tel: (802) 773 8930; Fax: (802) 773 6993
info@tuttlepublishing.com; www.tuttlepublishing.com

Japan
Tuttle Publishing
Yaekari Building, 3rd Floor
5-4-12 Osaki, Shinagawa-ku
Tokyo 141-0032
Tel: 81 (3) 5437 0171; Fax; (81) 3 5437 0755
sales@tuttle.co.jp; www.tuttle.co.jp

Asia Pacific
Berkeley Books Pte Ltd
3 Kallang Sector #04-01
Singapore 349278
Tel: (65) 6741 2178; Fax: (65) 6741 2179
inquiries@periplus.com.sg; www.tuttlepublishing.com

TUTTLE PUBLISHING® is a registered trademark of Tuttle Publishing, a division of Periplus Editions (HK) Ltd.